MY FAVORITE ILLUSTRATION

by

CARL G. JOHNSON

BAKER BOOK HOUSE
Grand Rapids, Michigan

Second printing, February 1975

PHOTOLITHOPRINTED BY CUSHING - MALLOY, INC.
ANN ARBOR, MICHIGAN, UNITED STATES OF AMERICA
1975

PREFACE

"Illustrations, like windows, let light into the chambers of the mind. Mere bald statements are soon forgotten, but an apt illustration sticks in the soul like a hook in a fish's mouth." So said "The Prince of Preachers," Charles H. Spurgeon. In his book, *Lectures to My Students,* he devotes ninety-five pages to the subject of illustrations. In the last five chapters in this book, he instructs preachers concerning: 1) "Illustrations in Preaching"; 2) "Anecdotes from the Pulpit"; 3) "The Uses of Anecdotes and Illustrations"; 4) "Where Can We Find Anecdotes and Illustrations?" and 5) "The Sciences as Sources of Illustration."

Henry Ward Beecher has pointed out that illustrations serve a seven-fold purpose:
1. They assist argument.
2. They help the hearer to remember.
3. They stimulate the imagination.
4. They rest the audience.
5. They provide for various classes of hearers.
6. They bridge difficult places.
7. They enforce the truth.

Dr. Harry Ironside, of whom Dr. Wilbur M. Smith stated, "The man that used illustrations perfectly and pointedly was Dr. Harry Ironside," wrote in the Preface of his book, *Illustrations of BIBLE Truth*: "Some object to the use of anecdotes of any kind in preaching and teaching, and think all that is needed is the unfolding of the truth. But most minds are so constituted that they need illustrations to enable them readily to grasp the full import of the message. Our Lord Himself used this method continually and in this, as in other things, He has left us an example, 'that ye should follow His steps.' "

A few months ago, I was driving to Illinois for an evangelistic meeting. Frequently as I drive I pray, and as I was praying and thinking, the thought came to me: "Why not write to about one hundred well-known speakers and ask them for their favorite illustrations?" As I continued to pray and think about this, I wrote Baker Book House concerning the idea of getting a favorite illustration from a number of these men, compiling and editing them, and having them published. They agreed that a book like this would be very helpful to pastors, evangelists, speakers, and writers, and encouraged me to proceed with this project.

I wrote to 142 speakers who are well known, told them about the proposed book, and asked each one of them to submit an illustration for use. Many of them were very gracious and cooperative. Some of them, because of pressing duties, or being out of the country, were not able to respond. A few did not care to respond. Quite a few of them had difficulty in selecting their favorite illustration. Evangelist Robert L. Sumner wrote in regard to this: "As well ask a farmer which raindrop falling on his thirsty wheat field is his favorite, or ask an astronomer to name his favorite body in the Milky Way, or ask a sea captain to identify his favorite ocean wave, or ask the librarian at the Library of Congress to name the volume housed in that archive which is his favorite — as to ask a preacher to name his favorite illustration."

I wish to thank every speaker who cooperated to make this book possible, and I pray that much blessing and fruit will come from these illustrations.

I have had a rewarding time compiling, editing, and giving titles to most of these illustrations. I have even included one of my favorite illustrations. They are now sent forth with the earnest prayer that God will use them to:

> assist argument
> help the hearer to remember
> stimulate the imagination
> rest the audience
> provide for various classes of hearers
> bridge difficult places
> enforce the truth
> and above all, bring glory to God.

CARL G. JOHNSON

CONTENTS

The Favorite Illustration of:

"WHAT IF WE DON'T LIKE IT?"

Some people worry about everything. Something *might* go wrong. The nice thing *may not* come. Tops in this pattern of thinking is the remark made by my father-in-law shortly before he died at the age of ninety-two. My wife had just conveyed the news to him that he would soon be going to heaven. She had sought to comfort him by telling him that we would all be joining him there soon. Then his lifelong propensity for worry came through. He said, "What if we don't like it?"

The Favorite Illustration of
ROGER J. ANDRUS, President
Calvary Bible College
Kansas City, Missouri

THE POWER OF THE BLOOD OF CHRIST

It was Charles G. Finney who told this story. He was holding a revival in Detroit. One night as he started to walk into the church, a man came up to him and asked, "Are you Dr. Finney?"

"Yes."

"I wonder if you will do me a favor. When you get through tonight, will you come home with me and talk to me about my soul?"

"Gladly. You wait for me." Finney walked inside. Some of the men stopped him.

"What did the man want, Brother Finney?"

"He wanted me to go home with him."

"Don't do it."

"I am sorry, but I promised and I shall go with him." When the service was over, Finney started for the door. The man was waiting, took his arm, and said, "Come with me."

They walked three or four blocks, turned into a side street, walked down an alley, and at the second house the man stopped.

"Stay here a minute, Brother Finney."

He reached into his pocket, pulled out a key, unlocked the door, turned to the preacher and said, "Come in." Mr. Finney walked into the room. There was a carpet on the floor, a fireplace, a desk, a swivel chair and two armchairs — nothing else. There was a tin partition around the room except for where the fireplace was. Finney turned around. The man had locked the door, had reached into his back pocket, had pulled out a revolver and was holding it in his hand.

"I don't intend to do you any harm," he said. "I just want to ask you some questions. Did you mean what you said in your sermon last night?"

"What did I say? I have forgotten."

"You said, 'The blood of Jesus Christ cleanses us from all sin.' "

Finney said, "Yes, God says so."

The man said, "Brother Finney, you see this revolver? It is mine. It has killed four people. Two of them were killed by me, two of them by my bartender in a brawl in my saloon. Is there hope for a man like me?"

Finney said, "God says, 'The blood of Jesus Christ his Son cleanseth us from all sin.' "

The man said, "Brother Finney, another question. Behind this partition is a saloon. I own it, everything in it. We sell every kind of liquor to anyone who comes along. Many, many times I have taken the last penny out of a man's pocket, letting his wife and children go hungry. Many times women have brought their babies here and pleaded with me not to sell any more booze to their husbands, but I have driven them out and kept right on with the whiskey selling. Is there hope for a man like me?"

Finney said, "God says, 'The blood of Jesus Christ his Son cleanseth us from all sin.' "

"Another question, Brother Finney. In back of this other partition is a gambling joint, and it is as crooked as sin, as crooked as Satan. There isn't a decent wheel in the whole place. It is all loaded and crooked. If a man leaves the saloon with some money left in his pocket we take his money away from him in there. Men have gone out of that gambling place to commit suicide when their money and perhaps entrusted funds were all gone. Is there any hope for a man like me?"

Finney said, "God says, 'The blood of Jesus Christ his Son cleanseth us from all sin.' "

"One more question, and I'll let you go. When you walk out of this alley, you turn to the right toward the street, look across the street, and there you will see a two-story brownstone house. It is my home. I own it. My wife is there, and my eleven-year-old child, Margaret. Thirteen years ago I went to New York on business. I met a beautiful girl. I lied to her. I told her I was a stock broker. She married me. I brought her here. When she found out my business it broke her heart. I have made life a hell on earth for her. I have come home drunk, beaten her, abused her, locked her out, made her life more miserable than that of any brute beast. About a month ago I went home one night drunk, mean, miserable. My wife got in the way somehow, and I started beating her. My daughter threw herself between us. I slapped that girl across the face and knocked her against a red-hot stove. Her arm is burned from shoulder to wrist. It will never look like anything decent. Brother Finney, is there hope for a man like me?"

Finney got hold of that man's shoulders, shook him, and said, "O son, what a black story you have to tell! But God says, 'The blood of Jesus Christ his Son cleanseth us from all sin.' "

The man said, "Thank you. Thank you very much. Pray for me. I am coming to church tomorrow night."

Finney went about his business. The next morning, about seven o'clock, the saloon keeper started to cross the street leaving his office. His necktie was awry. His face was dusty, sweaty, tear stained. He was shaking, rocking as though he were drunk. Earlier he had used the swivel chair to smash the mirror, the fireplace, the desk, and the other chairs. He had smashed the partition on each side. Every bottle and barrel and bar and mirror in that saloon was shattered and broken. The sawdust was swimming in a terrible mixture of beer, gin, whiskey, and wine. In the gambling establishment the tables were broken up and the dice and cards were smoldering in the fireplace. Now he staggered across the street, walked up the stairs of his home, and sat down heavily in the chair in his room. His wife called the little girl. "Maggie, run upstairs and tell Daddy breakfast is ready." The girl walked slowly up the stairs. Half afraid, she stood in the doorway and said, "Daddy, Mamma said breakfast was ready and she wants you to come down."

"Maggie darling, Daddy doesn't want any breakfast."

That little girl didn't walk; she flew down the stairs. "Mamma, Daddy said, 'Maggie darling,' and he didn't — "

"Maggie, you didn't understand. You go back upstairs and tell Daddy to come down." Maggie went back upstairs with the mother following her. The man looked up as he heard the child's step and said, "Maggie, come here."

Shyly, frightened, in a tremble, the little girl walked up to him. He lifted her, put her on his knee, pressed his face against her breast, and wept. The wife, standing in the door, didn't understand what had happened. After awhile he noticed her and said, "Wife, come here." He sat her down on his other knee, threw his big man's arms around those two whom he loved, whom he had so fearfully abused, lowered his face between them, and sobbed until the room almost shook with the impact of his emotion.

After some minutes he controlled himself, looked up into the faces of his wife and girl, and said, "Wife, daughter, you needn't be afraid of me any more. God has brought you a new man, a new daddy, home today."

That same night the man, his wife, and their child walked down the aisle of the church, gave their hearts to Christ and joined the church.

> The Favorite Illustration of
> HYMAN APPELMAN
> Kansas City, Missouri

ASHAMED AT HIS COMING

Perhaps we are living in the holy hush that precedes Christ's return. Therefore, we should be living soberly, righteously, and godly in this present age, looking for the blessed hope and the glorious appearing of our great God and Saviour Jesus Christ.

Early in my life I had an unusual experience which illustrates this truth. I was born in a little village way down East, the last child of a family of ten. Mother died when I was not quite six, and after her death the family broke up and moved to the cities of Boston and New York.

I was left alone with Father who, while hardworking and a generous provider for his family, nevertheless was a man of periodic harshness, and I suffered much from severe whippings and ill treatment.

My eldest brother who lived in New York had promised Mother the night she died that he would do his best to look after me; for Mother had given me to the Lord for His ministry. When he heard that I was being ill-treated he wrote to a schoolteacher friend who was a neighbor, and had her ask me if I would run away from home and come to New York to live with him.

I replied that I would be glad to go and live with him. It was arranged that Brother should come from New York to Boston and from there to St. John, New Brunswick, and then to Moncton on Labor Day and I was to come from the little village of Shediac, my home, to meet him there.

How long the summer seemed, waiting for Labor Day and his coming! But finally the eve of my departure came. Ordinarily I went barefoot all summer and wore few dress-up clothes except on Sunday, but I really prepared to meet my brother.

You see, he was a big "Abraham Lincoln" sort of fellow with a very kind heart, and I loved him greatly and wanted to make a good impression upon him when I met him. I was hungry for love, for I had been badly treated. If I was all dressed up, I reasoned, and my face was clean and my hair brushed, he would be so glad to see me that he'd give me a big hug and plant a kiss on my cheek.

So on the eve of Labor Day before I went to bed I got out a cheap little suit that Father had bought me, shined my shoes and prepared for the next day. Since I was running away from home, I did not let either my father or my step-mother know what I planned to do. They thought I was taking a brief trip to Moncton (some seventeen miles away) with other boys for a Labor Day celebration, and that I would be back that night.

I did not say good-bye to them, but with the pagan heart of a boy I said farewell to my bulldog and wept over his battle-scarred head with the realization that I never would see him again. Boarding the train for Moncton I saw it crowded with youngsters like myself who were filled with holiday spirit, but I did not participate in it because I had one objective: meeting my brother in Moncton.

I would arrive about eleven o'clock and he would get in from the south about four; then we were to take the train to St. John and proceed from there to Boston and New York. The schoolteacher through whom we had carried on our secret correspondence was also on the train to see that my brother and I got together.

As we arrived in Moncton and were standing about the depot platform, suddenly we heard the sound of a bugle and the roll of drums. All of us youngsters gave a shout and ran to the place from which the sound came. We discovered a gorgeous Labor Day parade just starting!

After the passing of the years I can't recall much except that there was a band and a drum major with a high "busby" and baton and a prancing step. There were bunting-covered floats and all the paraphernalia of a parade. How my heart leaped at the sight of it!

A group of us boys watched it go by, and then — (it must have been a short parade) we went to another street corner and watched it go by again, and then at another corner, and so on and on until about two o'clock in the afternoon when the parade was over. What happened in the meantime I do not recall, but some time after four o'clock I found myself back at the depot still talking about how marvelous the parade was and eating peanuts and popcorn in celebration.

Suddenly a heavy hand was on my shoulder and turning around I looked up into the face of the schoolteacher who was to see to it that I met my brother. She said, "Willie, where have you been? Your brother has arrived and he's up at my brother's house. You are supposed to take the six o'clock train to Boston tonight."

Then she gave me a searching look that took in every aspect of my appearance, and exclaimed, "My goodness, but you are dirty! What happened to you?"

Well, I was dirty. There had been a typical Labor Day-haze in the morning, soft drizzle at noon, then several downpours followed by sunshine. All this had happened during the parade, but we youngsters paid no attention. What mattered a little rain!

The streets were not paved in those days and we did not stay on the sidewalk but splashed through the mud. They told me afterward I was a mess. The cheap little suit had gotten wet and had shrunk grotesquely around me. All the polish was off my shoes, and I was splashed with mud from head to foot.

When the school teacher called attention to my condition, my soul was gripped with guilt. You see, I had planned to make a splendid appearance before my brother at his coming. And when I thought of my woebegone and disheveled appearance, I was sick. If I had done what my heart dictated I would have run away and hidden and not even met my brother after all those days of waiting!

However, the good woman took me by the hand, led me up the street to her brother's house, and opened the front door. I stepped into the living room where my tall brother was pacing back and forth. When he heard the door close he wheeled around quickly and his blue eyes became as wide as saucers. Then he began to scold me, for he was nervous and upset.

"Boy, where have you been?" he angrily asked. "I've been worried sick! And my, you look like a wet dog!"

Then he stopped his scolding and came slowly toward me. Suddenly he stopped and looked at me. There I stood — an underfed, undersized, dirty little lonesome boy with tears welling up in my eyes. That brother has long since gone to be with the Lord, but I'll never forget how he took me in his arms, wet and dirty as I was, gave me the hug that I hungered for, and planted a kiss on my cheek. He took me to Boston to see a brother and sister there, and then on to New York to live with him a much better life than I had known before.

I'm sure the illustration is clear. We talk much about the coming of Christ, but what of our lives? If He came today would we be ashamed before Him at His coming?

Do you remember when you gave your heart to Jesus how you rejoiced in His presence, and then when you learned that

He is coming again and you would see Him face to face, how your heart leaped for joy.

But then came the parade! You know what it was. There are different parades in the lives of different people. With some it is the cares of this world, with others the deceitfulness of riches. The parade to some is a thousand lives out of step with the love of Christ.

Whatever it was, you know that today your garments are spotted with the world, and unless you get back close to Him you will be ashamed before Christ at His coming.

The Favorite Illustration of
WILLIAM WARD AYER, Executive Director
Ayerow Christian Projects, Inc.
St. Petersburg, Florida

"THE UNDEFINABLE, INDESCRIBABLE LOVE OF GOD"

No one can estimate nor express the limitless love of God for a lost world. As I write these words I find myself in the same astounding situation Will Snow did the first time he saw the Pacific Ocean. Snow, a forty-three-year-old Zyante Indian from northern California, had been chosen to be trained for a place of leadership among the Zyantes by the late Dr. Harry Rimmer, scientist and Christian apologist. Snow had never seen an automobile, a train, electric lights, a city, anything remotely resembling civilization when Rimmer chose him for training. He simply was an Indain from the deep forests of the northern California mountains.

One day Dr. Rimmer took Snow to San Francisco, then on to the Pacific Ocean. The sight of that sea staggered the Indian's imagination. He wanted to know the name of the "lake." The largest lake he had ever seen was Clear Lake back home. Will had canoed and fished for blackfish on it. Rimmer replied, "Will, this is not a lake, but it is an ocean — the Pacific Ocean."

Snow nodded. "How big is it?"

Dr. Rimmer knew the answer: its area, width, depth; but how could he explain these figures to an ignorant Indian? The facts would mean nothing to a man who had known only lakes,

rivers, streams, forests. So, he suggested, "Will, you kr
Clear Lake?"

"Yes."

"Will, can you imagine ten Clear Lakes in one place?"

"Maybe."

"Will, can you imagine one hundred Clear Lakes in one place?"

"Too much," replied the Indian, "You got that much in this ocean?"

Rimmer responded, "That much would only be a drop, Will, if you took it out of the ocean."

The Indian shook his head. Then he asked, "Who drinks it?"

"No one — it is salty."

The Indian stooped down, tasted it, spat it out with a wry face. He went farther down the beach and tested it there. The result was the same. He waded out in it. Again he spat it out. By now he believed his teacher.

Later in the day Dr. Rimmer was watching Will. Fascinated, amazed by that ocean, he studied it, waded in it, thrilled to it. It was about time for them to leave when Rimmer saw Snow go down to the ocean again. This time he had a pint bottle. He bent over, filling it with water. "What are you going to do with it, Will?" The Indian held up his filled bottle. "I'm going to take it home. My people will never believe what I have seen today. I want them to see for themselves."

We smile at the innocence and ignorance of this poor Indian who thought that a pint bottle could capture the vastness, the limitlessness, the surging surf, the thrilling, stirring emotions, the sights and smells of that greatest of oceans. Just so I acknowledge my poverty as I pen these paragraphs. I know the best I can bring you is a similar pint-sized picture of the limitless love of God. My finite brain and feeble, beggaring vocabulary cannot fathom nor frame the language necessary to describe to you the inexhaustible depths and dimensions of divine love. Even the apostle Paul, peerless preacher that he was, could not define that love. The best he could utter as an expression of that unlimited love was:

" . . . that ye . . . may be able to comprehend with all saints what is the breadth, and length, and depth, and height; and to know the love of Christ which passeth knowledge . . ." (Eph. 3:17-19).

Indescribable, undefinable, past knowledge is God's love, yet, even a casual reading of that passage shows that God's love may not be adequately defined; it can be definitely illustrated because it has breadth, it has length, it has depth, it has height, it has four dimensions, it has four arms — the arms of the cross sunk in a socket on Calvary's hill and Jesus Christ, God's Son, stretched out, smitten, sacrificed, shedding His blood, the Substitute for sinners, slain on that cross.

My prayer is that every reader will believe the precious promise of God's great love and receive the so-great salvation provided in the sacrifice of His Son as penned in John 3:16, "For God so loved the world, that He gave His only begotten Son, that whosoever believeth in Him should not perish, but have everlasting life."

The Favorite Illustration of
FRED BARLOW, Sunday School Consultant
Regular Baptist Press
Des Plaines, Illinois

SEEING THE HARVEST INSTEAD OF THE FENCES

My wife, Betty, and I visited the farm lands of Scotland while conducting evangelistic meetings in nearby Edinburgh. We were impressed with the picturesque countryside and the beautiful little farms or ranchettes. We were particularly impressed with the stone fences that separated these little farms. In fact, we remember posing for a picture leaning against one of these fences of stone.

Some years later we returned to Scotland with our two daughters. As the plane was coming in for a landing in Glasgow, we looked out over the countryside and, to our surprise, we could see no fences. I remarked to the stewardess of our impressions of a few years earlier. She commented, "Oh, you must have come in the spring when the grain was short. Now it is harvesttime and the grain has grown higher than the fences and because of the ripened grain you cannot see the dividing fences."

I thought what a difference it would make if all of us, as God's children, could see the harvest instead of the fences that divide us. In this day, just before the final storm breaks upon the world, it behooves us to get our eyes off that which divides us and see the opportunities of reaping the golden harvest.

The Favorite Illustration of
CHARLES E. BLAIR, Pastor
Calvary Temple
Denver, Colorado

"AT LAST I HAVE FOUND PEACE"

On one occasion after a morning service in St. Louis, a splendid-looking young man came to me and said, "When you gave the invitation to accept Christ, I was one who should have raised his hand, but I did not." We went to my study where it was my happy privilege to point this earnest seeker to the Saviour. He then told me how God had led him to our church.

While in boarding school years before, his faith had been shaken; and later, at the university, it was completely shattered. While there, he fell heir to a philosophy of determinism: one can get what he wants if he wants it badly enough. Since his university days, he had sought in many directions to find peace for his soul.

Several days before, he had arrived in St. Louis on business. Sunday morning he sat in his hotel room, thinking of his wife and two little children who would be in church as usual. Frequently, they had invited him to go, but he had always proffered the same reply, "Maybe next week."

As he pondered, he considered the importance of a father's example to his growing children. Many thoughts ran through his mind. "Perhaps I should go to church," he reflected. "Today might be a good time to start. No — what would be the use? — There is no God. But yet, maybe there is!"

He decided to put God to the test. A drenching rain was falling. He knelt and prayed something like this: "God — if there is a God — prove yourself and make it stop raining so I can go to church and find faith." Glancing through the window, he noticed that it seemed to be raining harder than ever. He shrugged his shoulders and sat down to read. Suddenly, however, the sun peeped through the clouds and the rain stopped.

He dashed for his car and drove off in search of a church. Within moments he found ours, and about an hour later, God completely answered that businessman's humble prayer, for he found faith in Jesus Christ. At our Wednesday evening prayer service, he told of his experience on the previous Lord's Day. At the conclusion he paused and then said quietly, "At last I have found peace!"

How thrilling it is to know that all who receive Christ have peace with God instantly. Christ, the Person of peace, was born into this world to provide eternal peace for all who trust in Him.

Have you experienced His peace by receiving Him, the Lord Jesus Christ?

The Favorite Illustration of
J. ALLEN BLAIR, Director
Glad Tidings, Inc.
Charlotte, North Carolina

"I'M STILL WALKIN' WITH THE LORD"

The Bible says in II Corinthians 5:17, "Therefore if any man be in Christ, he is a new creature: old things are passed away; behold, all things are become new." The Bible says that the new birth is a new creation.

In May of 1940 I conducted a two-week meeting in Cravette, Arkansas, a small town in the Ozark Mountains. One day while walking downtown with a member of the church I saw a seventy-five-year-old man sitting on a wooden bench in front of a produce store, whittling on a stick and squirting tobacco juice into the street. I asked the church member, "Who is that man?" He answered, "That's old Jack Lakin. He's a drunkard and a gambler. He's the meanest man in town. You'd better leave old Jack alone. He'll only cuss you." I told the church member that I would see him later, and I walked across the street and introduced myself to Jack Lakin. I sat down on the bench beside him and told him that I too had been a drunkard and a gambler and that God saved me in answer to a Christian mother's prayer. With a look of interest he said to me, "You're the preacher over at the tabernacle, aren't you?" I answered, "Yes." He said, "Preacher, I'm gonna come to the meetin' and hear you make a talk."

And Jack Lakin came to that meeting. And when I gave the invitation for sinners to come to Christ, Jack Lakin came down the aisle and went down upon his knees and turned from sin to God. He believed on the Lord Jesus Christ and was saved. He was born again. He became a new creation.

In August of 1949 I was driving to Winona Lake, Indiana, from meetings in California. The Lord laid it upon my heart to stop at Gravette, Arkansas, which wasn't too far off my route, and visit some of the people who were saved in that meeting in 1940. I arrived in Gravette one evening at dusk and rented a tourist cabin. The owner of the cabins told me that the Baptist church was having a tent meeting. I took my bags into the cabin and then drove down to the meeting. The evangelist was preaching, so I slipped into the back row of benches and sat down beside Tom Haywood, a Christian businessman. After the meeting was dismissed with prayer my friend Tom grabbed my arm and said, "Come with me. I want to show you something." He took me down the aisle to the front row of benches and pointed out Jack Lakin, eighty-four years of age, standing with a Bible under his arm and the light of heaven upon his face. I walked over to him and took him by the hand and said, "Jack, you don't know me." Those blue eyes, dimmed with age, scanned my face for only a moment, then lit up with recognition. He answered, "I shore do! You're Charlie Boren! It's shore good to see you, Charlie! I'm still walkin' with the Lord!" And Jack walked with the Lord to the end. In 1952 I was in meetings near Gravette and visited Jack. I found him on his deathbed. He gripped my hand and assured me that he would soon see the Saviour who loved him and died for him. "Therefore if any man be in Christ, he is a new creature: old things are passed away; behold, all things are become new" (II Cor. 5:17).

The Favorite Illustration of
CHARLES BOREN, Evangelist
Winona Lake, Indiana

LITTLE ACTS OF LOVE

" . . . ye yourselves are taught of God to love one another" (I Thess. 4:9).

True love reveals itself not so much in a great outward show of emotion, but rather in a thousand small acts of devotion and consideration. It is by these that we manifest our true colors and display our real attitudes.

When I was a little boy about three and a half years old, I knew that my father was extremely fond of black walnuts. We did not often get them, so when I found one upon the street I was delighted! My first thought was to have my mother crack it so that I could eat it myself, but then my great love for Father took over. I saved it until he came home that evening. It was my custom to wait until I saw him come around the corner and then rush to meet him. I would throw my small arms around his one leg and thus, standing on his foot, would be swung along with his powerful stride until we got home. All the way he would be patting my head and smiling and talking to me. This night I presented him with the walnut and said, "Here, Papa, I've been saving it all day — just for you!" I thought it very strange that he did not want to crack it and eat it, and it was not until thirty years later that I found it again after he had left us for the heavenly mansions. It was in a place by itself in his desk. Mother told me he considered it such a sincere token of my deep affection for him that he wanted to keep it as a memento.

Don't delay performing even the smallest act of love today; believe me, it is sorely needed and will be much appreciated. What is more, it will be richly rewarded by the Lord. Do not keep the alabaster boxes of your love and tenderness sealed up until your friends are dead. Fill their lives with sweetness now. By the power of the Holy Spirit, let us exchange our self-centered attitudes for heartfelt words and deeds which will manifest that we love the brethren "with a pure heart fervently" (I Peter 1:22)!

Breathe on me, Breath of God,
Fill me with life anew,
That I may love as Thou dost love,
And do what Thou wouldst do.
— E. Hatch

When God measures a man, He puts the tape around the heart — not the head!

The Favorite Illustration of
HENRY G. BOSCH, Editor
Our Daily Bread
Radio Bible Class
Grand Rapids, Michigan

"THAT REVIVAL IS DRYING UP THE WHOLE COUNTY"

During one of my revivals in south Texas I was led to the home of an outstanding businessman. He was the owner of two restaurants.

We found him at home taking a nap. Even though we had disturbed him, he was very gracious. I approached him with this question, "We are sorry to disturb you but we wanted to make sure you were on your way to heaven. If you died today, would you go to heaven? Have you been saved?"

He replied, "No, I have never been saved." His answer was not ugly. The conversation was left open for more probing by the Holy Spirit.

I continued, "Wouldn't you like to know today that you were saved and you do have a home in heaven?"

Again the reply came, "Yes, I would like to know, but I don't want to be a hypocrite about it."

"You don't have to be a hypocrite. Let's see what the Bible says," I replied. I began immediately to show him in Romans 5:12 that sin came into the world by Adam. Man is condemned because of sin and is facing the second death. Then showing him other verses I went down the plan of salvation. After a little bit I began to question him, "Do you believe God's Word?" The answer was affirmative. Then I asked, "Do you believe that God will do what He says?" "Yes, I do," was his reply.

In a few minutes we were on our knees in prayer. He claimed God's promise to save him if he would believe in Jesus and receive Him. His sins were washed away and sweet joy came flooding into his soul.

Then I received a shock. I learned that he sold beer in both his restaurants and that he gambled heavily. We discussed this and I told him, "You're saved now; however, if I were you I would not be baptized and join the church until I quit selling beer. You see, it would ruin the testimony of the church."

He did not have a lot to say. He seemed a little stunned. Sometimes new Christians do not understand that the church body is to be separated from sin. I then said to him, "I will be looking for you this week at the revival services. I hope that you will begin to follow Christ and come for baptism." For several days he did not show up. My heart was heavy for him. I knew what a terrible price he was going to have to pay. Would he do it, or would he renounce Christ and go back to the world?

Finally my heart became so heavy that I had to pay him another visit. I went to the cafe this time. He seemed to ignore me at first. I thought, "Well, he is going to drop by the wayside. He has decided not to pay the price." Men were sitting around me eating their meals. In a few minutes he came to where I was sitting. "Hello, Brother Joe. It is good to see you. What are you fellows doing here?"

I answered, "Oh, I thought we'd just drop by and see how you were making out since Jesus saved you."

He turned, picked up a menu and opened it. "Let me show you what I've been doing!"

"I don't see anything. What have you been doing?" I asked. He then pointed to the bottom of the menu and there in plain type-written words I saw "Jesus loves you. Won't you think of Him today?" How wonderful! Only about three days old in the Lord and he has already begun to witness in print to all of his customers. Sometimes young Christians are much more fervent in their witness for Christ than older Christians.

"Do you know what I have been doing all day?" he asked. I had no idea, so I replied, "No, what have you been doing?"

"Well, I have poured out about seventy cases of beer. I

have called the beer agent and asked him to pick up all the rest. I am out of the beer business," he said.

We rejoiced together, thanking God for such tremendous faith. We said good-bye and started to leave. As I went out the door I noticed some men had come and were beginning to cut off the neon signs at the restaurant that read, "Beer." Two men were standing with great concern watching the operation, and one of these men said, "I don't know what is going to happen next. That revival is drying up the whole county."

I remarked, "Praise God. I pray to God that it will dry up all the country, including the entire United States!" Since they did not know me they looked in amazement. They just could not believe that anyone would be in agreement in stopping the sale of beer for any reason.

The restaurant owner came on to church and was baptized. I do not know what he is doing now, but I thank God that Christ caused him to take his stand and become a daily witness in the area.

The Favorite Illustration of
JOE BOYD, Evangelist
Hammond, Indiana

NO ONE TOO DIFFICULT, NO ONE TOO HARD

I was invited for a revival meeting in the Calvary Baptist Church in Arcadia, Nebraska, through the invitation of the pastor, Rev. Chuck Ver Straten. When I got to Arcadia, the temperature stood at ten below zero and the snow was deep.

They had arranged for a cottage prayer meeting at ten o'clock on the Monday morning after we started on Sunday night. We had difficulty in getting the car started because of the extreme cold. Finally we got the preacher's car going and arrived at the prayer meeting about ten minutes late. In the process of praying around the circle one of the men prayed very earnestly for a man by the name of Jake Greenland. On the way home the pastor of the church said, "If that fellow Jake Greenland comes to the revival meeting, the church will fall in"; and he related to me the notorious character of Jake Greenland.

He had the reputation for being a hard, two-fisted, western-pioneer-type person. Although he was successful in farming and the raising of cattle, he was not respected in the community.

The second night of the revival meeting a tall, husky, and rugged man came into the auditorium just about the time the song service started. With him was his wife; she appeared tense and timid. Their late entrance immediately drew my attention but I had no idea who they were.

Later the pastor asked me, "Did you notice that man that came in late? Do you have any idea who he was?" It was then that I learned that it was Jake Greenland. The preacher predicted, "He will never come back again; that strong sermon on hell will knock him clear out of the ball park . . . he will never come back again!"

However, the next night Jake Greenland was back in the audience, accompanied by his wife and daughter. I was disheartened as I watched them leave so quickly after the service — without Christ. But the third or fourth night he returned. I preached and then gave the invitation. The first one to walk down the aisle was Jake Greenland. It literally upset the remainder of the service. Overwhelmed, the man who had prayed for him wept. Sobs came from the people in the church who knew of Jake Greenland's character and reputation. Jake came right down the aisle to the front of the church, knelt down, and really got right with God. If that were the end of the story that would be thrilling enough . . . but that is not the end of the story.

About three years later I was invited back to the same church for a second revival meeting. The first man to greet me at the door of the church the first night was Jake Greenland. It was obvious that he was no longer just a spectator or someone for whom to pray. Jake Greenland was the head usher and one of the most active men in the church. His wife was now a gracious, kind, smiling person. Having lunch in their home was a real delight and treat. His attitude was gracious and spiritual . . . an example of God's marvelous power in convicting and converting a lost sinner.

I tell this story to illustrate the fact that we need to pray for our loved ones. There is no one too difficult, no one too hard; and even though others may not have too much faith in the power of God, God hears and answers prayer. This is one of the most thrilling experiences of my life and in my ministry.

The Favorite Illustration of
HOMER BRITTON, Evangelist
Chattanooga, Tennessee

THE WIFE IS "TO PLAY SECOND FIDDLE"

My favorite illustration, probably, is the simple explanation of the words, "obedient to their own husbands," in Titus 2:5.

The word *obedient* (*huptasso*) means "to arrange oneself under," or "to take a lesser place." In the colloquial rendering it might be rendered "to play second fiddle."

When one considers what happens when the second or harmony part is added it presents a lovely picture — the wife standing alongside her husband, in her God-given place as his help-meet, endeavoring to make harmony out of every circumstance. If the husband is in a minor key she harmonizes in a major key and soon things are better. If his demands are a strident, rash tone her mild, sweet harmonious influence will soothe and quiet. To be an obedient wife in this sense is a wonderful challenge to a Christian woman.

The Favorite Illustration of
FRED R. BROCK, JR., President
Western Baptist Bible College
Salem, Oregon

"WHEN JESUS GOES THROUGH HE TAKE CUDJO THROUGH"

Upon graduation from college in 1933, I went directly to Mobile, Alabama, to begin my ministry of evangelism. Upon my arrival one of my dearest friends, who had graduated earlier and now lived there, wanted to show me the sights. He asked me if I had seen Cudjo. I asked, "What is that?" He answered, "Cudjo is not a what but a whom." I then inquired, "Who is that?"

My friend explained that Cudjo was the only black man still living who had crossed the ocean on a slave boat. I assured my friend that I wanted to see this man, so we drove out to his little cabin situated on a little knoll just outside the city limits. As we approached, we could see Cudjo sitting on the porch rocking. He stood up as we approached. With a big smile on his face he assured us we were welcome. He was a stately man with hair and beard as white as snow.

After a long visit we prepared to leave. I asked Cudjo if he was saved. He assured me that he was and I asked him how he knew. He said he was a good man. I assured him that he could be a good man and not be saved. He replied, "Oh, white boy wants me to tell him *why* I know I saved." "Yes," I said, "That is what I want to know, how do you know you are saved?" He said, "Cudjo show you why he know." He looked around until he found a little piece of string, then taking a handkerchief out of his pocket he held it up and tried to push the string through it. He looked at my friend and said, "Can you push string through handkerchief?" My friend assured him he couldn't. He looked at me and I shook my head. Then he said, "President of United States, biggest man in world, smartest man in world, he can't push it through!" We assured him that the president couldn't do it either. Then he said, "Cudjo can push it through." We asked him how he would do it. He said, "Cudjo get a needle. He put string in needle. He push needle through and string come through with it."

Then his eyes filled with tears and he lifted his face toward heaven. As I looked into that tear-stained face, I felt I had never seen a man closer to God than Old Cudjo Lewis, over a hundred years old, the last living slave who crossed the ocean on a slave boat. (An interview with Cudjo was later published in *Literary Digest*.) He said, "Jesus is the Needle, Cudjo is the string, Cudjo is in Jesus and when Jesus goes through He take Cudjo through." I said, "Praise God, if I live to be a thousand years old, I will never hear it any plainer than that." If you are in Christ you have life. "He that hath the Son hath life" (I John 5:12).

The Favorite Illustration of
FRED BROWN, Evangelist
Chattanooga, Tennessee

THE REMEDY

A skeptical doctor said to his Christian patient, "I could never understand saving faith. I believe in God and I suppose I believe in Jesus Christ — I am not conscious of any doubts. I believe that Jesus Christ was the Son of God, and I believe the Bible, yet I am not saved. What is the matter with me?"

"Well," said the patient, "a week ago I believed in you as a very skillful doctor. I believed that if I should get sick and put myself in your hands I would be healed. In other words, I trusted you. For two days now I have been taking some mysterious stuff out of a bottle. I don't know what it is, I don't understand it, but I am trusting in you. Now, whenever you turn to the Lord Jesus Christ and say, 'Lord Jesus, Christianity seems to me to be full of mysteries. I do not understand them, but I believe Thou art trustworthy and I trust Thee; I commit myself to Thee,' *that is faith.*"

A very simple thing, is it not? The faith of the patient did not heal him; it was the remedy that healed him; but the faith took the remedy!

The lost soul *must believe* the *testimony* of the Bible. "Christ died for our sins." The lost soul *must trust* the *promise* of Jesus, "Him that cometh to me I will in no wise cast out." And the lost soul *must accept Christ* into his heart as God's gift for his salvation.

The Favorite Illustration of
RICHARD V. CLEARWATERS, Pastor
Fourth Baptist Church
Minneapolis, Minnesota

A CONVINCING TESTIMONY TO THE FAITHFULNESS OF GOD

When I was a student pastor in the city of Camden, New Jersey, there was an old lady in the congregation who lived with her brother, an ungodly man who ridiculed her faith.

Both were in their eighties. For many years she had claimed the promise of Acts 16:31 in prayer, believing that God would save this ungodly member of her household. One night he had a stroke, and the doctor said he would not live until morning. She called me in. Knowing how well she knew the Scriptures, I asked her what portion she would like to have me read to her brother. She said, "Please read Isaiah 53."

After making sure he could understand us, by the pressure of his hand and the movement of his eyes, I began reading. As I reached the sixth verse his body began to tremble, and I said to him, "We think you just now received Christ as your Saviour, and that you know you have become a child of God. If this is so, let your sister know by pressing her hand and blinking your eyes." His response left no doubt that God had answered her prayers as her brother listened to the wonderful words, "All we like sheep have gone astray; we have turned every one to his own way; and the Lord hath laid on him the iniquity of us all." She became a convincing testimony to the faithfulness of God to His praying saints.

That dying man was able to tell us what had happened to him. Who knows how many loved ones for whom Christians have prayed have been saved, like him, at the point of death, without being able to tell their families that their prayers were indeed answered?

The Favorite Illustration of
S. MAXWELL CODER,
Dean of Education, Emeritus
Moody Bible Institute
Chicago, Illinois

"WHERE WERE YOUR EYES?"

Tigranese, king of Armenia, was taken captive by a conquering Roman army. The defeated king, his wife, and all his children were brought before the Roman general for the sentence of death. Tigranese threw himself on his knees before the conqueror and pleaded for the lives of his family. He said to the victorious Roman: "Take me and do anything you like with me, but spare my wife and children." His appeal so moved the general that he set the entire family free. As they journeyed away from the Roman headquarters, Tigranese turned to his wife sitting by his side, and said, "What did you think of the Roman general?" She replied, "I never saw him." Tigranese exclaimed, "You never saw him! You were standing in his presence. Where were your eyes?" She said, "They were fixed upon the one who was willing to die for me. I saw no one else."

Were you there when they crucified my Lord?
　　Were you there?
Were you there when they crucified my Lord?
　　Were you there?
Oh, sometimes it makes me to tremble, tremble, tremble,
　　Were you there when they crucified my Lord?

What do you see when you look at the cross? We see our victory over sin, death, hell, and the grave. Through the veil of His flesh, torn asunder, we have our entrance into heaven. Sin no longer has dominion over us. The grave can no longer hold us. Hell no longer is a fear for us. We are more than conquerors through Him who loved us and gave Himself for us.

"O death, where is thy sting? O grave, where is thy victory? The sting of death is sin; and the strength of sin is the law. But thanks be to God, which giveth us the victory through our Lord Jesus Christ" (I Cor. 15:55-57). What do you see when you look at the cross?

God calls to our hearts:

> *Hoc feci pro te*
> *Quid facis pro me.*
> This have I done for thee.
> What hast thou done for me?

Surely, Lord, my life, my soul, my all belong to Thee.

> Was it for crimes that I have done
> 　　He groaned upon the tree?
> Amazing pity, grace unknown,
> 　　And love beyond degree!

> But drops of grief can ne'er repay

The debt of love I owe.
Here, Lord, I give myself away,
'Tis all that I can do.

— Isaac Watts

The Favorite Illustration of
W. A. CRISWELL, Pastor
First Baptist Church
Dallas, Texas

"I AIN'T GOT NO HOME"

It was late afternoon on a cold, windy, snowy November day, and I had headed my car south on Route 21, having finished my day of calling.

As it grew darker I turned on my car lights, and they emphasized a shabbily dressed man, half-heartedly "thumbing a ride," along the highway. His clothes were ragged, dirty, and surely insufficient for the weather. He acted as though he didn't expect anyone to pick him up, or perhaps it just didn't make much difference either way.

I very seldom pick up a hitch-hiker anymore, because of the many dangers involved, but the old fellow looked so pitiful, I pulled over and opened the door for him to get in.

I turned the heater up and he rubbed his cold hands together in appreciation, and thanked me for giving him a lift.

I introduced myself to him, and tried to engage him in conversation.

"Where are you going?" I asked.

"Oh, no place in particular," was the evasive answer.

I thought perhaps he was heading south for the winter, or trying to get to some particular destination before severe weather set in.

I tried again. "Where are you from?"

Again the answer came, as though from way back in the distant recesses of his mind, "Nowhere, really, I guess."

Finally, I asked, "Well, Friend, where is your home?"

He looked at me with a puzzled, quizzical look and said, "Home?"

"Yes," I said, "Home! Where is your home?"

He shook his head in sadness as he replied, "Home? I don't have a home!"

I supposed he thought I was trying to question him for other purposes, to determine if he were a criminal, a runaway from certain authorities, or something of this nature, so I explained again that I was a preacher, and only interested in him as a person whom I could possibly help.

Once more I gave it a try. "Don't you have a father, or mother somewhere? Don't you have a wife, or children? Isn't there somewhere you call 'home'?"

Then, once more, as in dejected finality, he replied, "No, I ain't got nobody. I ain't got no home!"

In the downtown area, I let him out where three highways joined, so that he might find another ride — to nowhere!

I headed my car west across town, pondering the thought, "No home!" I had never experienced being without a home. In less than five minutes I would pull into the driveway of a little place I call "home." Neither rich nor fancy, but "home." Soon, I would be in the kitchen with the good smells of "home cooking," and with the love of wife and family around me. Home! "Be it ever so humble, there's no place like home!"

My mind turned again to that poor tramp I had left standing on the corner pulling his too-thin overcoat about him, and clutching in the other hand some Gospel tracts I had given him after I had witnessed to him. "I ain't got no home!" No lamp in a window burning for him. No one wondering about him. No one who cared. He could crawl under a bridge or a railroad trestle at night and freeze to death to be found next spring, and no one would miss him, or mourn his passing. No home!

My mind turned to a passage of Scripture that described the unsaved as being without Christ, without God, without hope, and aliens and strangers from the covenants of promise (Eph. 2:11-13).

Oh, how tragic for many who walk the pathways of life, without a loved one, and without a home! How much more tragic for those who shall drift on out into eternity, lost, and without Christ, to forever be in the caverns of the damned, "aliens," and *homeless forever!*

In addition to all else that heaven will be for the redeemed, it will be *home!* Home with Christ, with loved ones, with the redeemed. Besides all else that hell is, it will be eternal separation from God, and His grace, without a "heavenly home," while eternal ages roll on!

The Favorite Illustration of
BRUCE CUMMONS, Pastor
Massillon Baptist Temple
Massillon, Ohio

YOUNG PEOPLE PRAYED AND GOD SENT REVIVAL

I recall an incident in which God answered a prayer and sent a mighty revival. A few years ago I was conducting a revival meeting in the great People's Church of Toronto, Canada, of which Dr. Oswald J. Smith was the pastor. I had also been in the church a year previously and had an engagement to return about a year later. Several outstanding evangelists had been in the church between my first meeting and my return. Moreover, just before I arrived they had closed a great missionary convention lasting for some two weeks. I wondered how we could maintain great crowds and how we could have many conversions since for many years Dr. Smith had brought to the church to conduct revivals some of the greatest evangelists in the world, including Gypsy Smith and others of his caliber.

We had good crowds and some conversions during the first week. On Sunday night, the middle Sunday night of the meeting, we had only about twelve or thirteen saved of an audience of some two thousand. My heart was burdened and broken. It seemed to me that we should have had many more. After the service, I went back into the pastor's study and sat there with a heavy heart. Someone came and said, "The young people are praying on the top floor of the church. They would like to have you join them."

There I saw thirty-four young people, many of them — I dare say most of them — in their teens. They were down on their knees crying to God to save souls and to send a great revival. I heard them weeping as if their hearts were broken. When one would finish praying another would speak and call the name of a brother, a sister, or a friend, and say, "Pray for him." Then they would begin to pray again.

This continued until nearly midnight. My heart was so blessed by their praying that I said, "Young people, let's meet every night and call on God to send a great revival. And especially let's pray for our youth service which is to be held next Friday night."

Every night a group of them met to pray. God gave a real revival that week. Friday came; it began to rain early in the morning and continued all day long. Late in the afternoon, near nighttime, I was burdened. I felt like crying out, "Oh, God, these young people have been praying all of the week for a great revival. Now it's raining and we cannot have a big crowd at this service. Certainly the high school students won't come through the rain. Lord, I don't understand it." But I was to see God work that night.

When I entered the church a little after seven o'clock the building was about three-fourths full, and most of those in the audience were high school students. By the time the service began the auditorium was fairly well filled, with high school and college students still in the majority. In spite of the rain they had come from all over the city of Toronto. That night the power of God fell on that audience. When the invitation was given, 252 people, most of them young people, walked down that aisle, many to be saved, and many others to take the vow of purity to stand against sin of all kinds and live for Christ.

It was a glorious sight. On the next Sunday night, the building was packed, and scores were standing. The young people sent a message up to the pulpit that read, "Brother Daniels, if it's all right with you, we'll go to the upper room and pray while you preach."

At no other time have I felt the power that I felt that night. It just seemed that I was wafted along on the wings of prayer. The power of God gripped me. I have never preached with greater ease. It seemed that I did not have to *preach* — there seemed to be a greater power uttering the words through me. That night you could have heard a pin drop throughout the service. When finally the invitation was given some fifty people, most of them adults, and many of them cultured people of that great city, walked down the aisle, weeping their way to God.

The Favorite Illustration of
E. J. DANIELS, President
Christ for the World, Inc.
Orlando, Florida

WEAK THROUGH THE FLESH

"For what the law could not do, in that it was weak through the flesh . . ." (Rom. 8:3a).

It was the late and beloved Bible teacher Dr. Wm. Pettingill who so vividly illustrated the truth of this verse by telling about one of his own personal experiences. He had been invited to the home of close friends for dinner. Wandering into the kitchen, Dr. Pettingill entered just as the hostess took a large fork and thrust it into a beautifully browned roast, and tried to lift it from the pan. So tender, however, was the meat, that the fork could not support it. It just went right through. Finally, after several attempts, she gave up, and taking a large spatula placed it under the roast and removed it in that way. Dr. Pettingill went on to say that the fork reminded him of the law and the roast portrayed man's sinful nature. Although the fork failed to lift the roast out of the kettle, *it was not the fault of the fork!* There was nothing wrong with it at all. It was a good strong one. The problem was in the meat. The fork was "weak" through the flesh. That's exactly what Paul was trying to say in Romans 8:3 when he spoke of "what the law could not do." God's law was perfect and good, but it could never save anyone simply because of the depravity of the human heart and the inability of sinful man to support it. For that very reason, "God sending his own Son in the likeness of sinful flesh, and for sin, condemned sin in the flesh: That the righteousness of the law might be fulfilled in us . . . " (Rom. 8:3b-4).

Salvation is not obtained by keeping the Ten Commandments, for "they that are in the flesh cannot please God." It is received by trusting Christ who alone fulfilled God's perfect law.

The Favorite Illustration of
RICHARD W. DE HAAN, Teacher
Radio Bible Class
Grand Rapids, Michigan

WILLING TO GO, EVEN TO THE "CORN FIELD"

I sat in the last bench of Moody Church and heard the choir sing and waited for the public speaker to preach so that I could learn more English. The late Paul Rader was pastor of the Moody Church at that time. The Holy Spirit began to speak to me and I saw that I was a lost sinner and I realized the need for Christ who died for a sinful world, including me. Yet I was not willing to accept Him as my personal Saviour as I was too much a part of the world and loved worldly things.

At the evening service, after a great evangelistic message, Mr. Rader invited those who wanted to accept the Lord as their personal Saviour to come to the altar. I answered that call and went forward. I knelt and wept before God, realizing I was a needy, lost sinner, without Christ. I accepted the Lord as my Saviour. This was a great day in my life: my spiritual birthday.

Then the Lord spoke to me definitely about consecrating my life fully to Him, so that I would be willing to go anywhere.

It is wonderful how the Spirit works although many times we cannot understand what ministers mean. The Holy Spirit corrects it and makes it right.

Six months after I was converted I attended a foreign missionary conference held in Moody Church conducted by Mr. Rader. He always talked about needing young people to give their lives for the foreign field. I didn't understand the word *foreign* and thought he said "corn field."

I was so willing to know and to do God's will. So when the invitation was given to go forward, I went, willing to go wherever God would lead, even to the "corn field." There I

39

consecrated and yielded my life to Jesus Christ, and told Him that I was willing to be what He wanted me to be. The Lord filled me with His Holy Spirit and gave me victory, a passion for lost souls, and a great vision for the people who are without Christ. Thank God, I have never stopped marching for Jesus, with the gospel, since my surrender to Him.

The Favorite Illustration of
PETER DEYNEKA, General Director
Slavic Gospel Association, Inc.
Chicago, Illinois

"GOOD NIGHT" OR "GOOD-BYE"

Some years ago a father, who had several sons and daughters and a wonderful Christian wife, lay dying of an incurable disease. All of the family except one son were very quickly contacted and came to the bedside of the dying father.

One son, who had resented the discipline of his parents and the deeply religious atmosphere of their home, had left home a few years before, angry with his parents and determined to live his own life. With the help of the Red Cross and other organizations, this wayward son was finally contacted and agreed to come home. He arrived only a few hours before his father slipped into eternity.

The father was conscious up until the very end, and shortly before his death, he called all of his family into his room and talked to them one by one.

He said to his wife, "Honey, you have been a wonderful mother and wife and the finest Christian woman I have ever known. I appreciate you more than words can express and wish to thank you for being what you are"; and then he smiled and looked into her face and said, "Good night, Honey."

Then, one by one, he called the other children to his bedside and expressed his appreciation for their fine Christian character, their love, and the wonderful care that had been bestowed upon him by them and each time he closed his conversation by smiling and looking into their face and saying, "Good night, Son" or, "Good night, Daughter." Finally he called the wayward son to his bedside and said, "Son, if I have ever failed you in any way, I am sorry. In some respects I think I have loved you almost more than the other children because of your nature." Then he looked up and said, "Daddy is dying now and will soon be home with his Lord, and as much as it hurts me, I must say good-bye."

The son fell on his knees and grabbed the old man in his arms and said, "Dad, you said good night to all the others; why did you say good-bye to me?"

The old man looked up with tears in his eyes and said, "Son, all the others know my Saviour, the Lord Jesus Christ. I have tried for years to lead you to know Him, but you have rejected Him. I will meet all the others in heaven, but I have no hope of ever meeting you again. Therefore it must be good-bye."

The boy began to weep and cried out, "Daddy, don't leave me like this! I, too, want to meet you in heaven."

With the last strength he had left in his body, the father pointed his son to the Lord Jesus Christ. Weeping upon his dying father's shoulders, the son cried out, "Father, I accept Him, I accept Him; He is my Saviour, too!"

The old man looked up and smiled and said, "Good night, Son," and then closed his eyes and slipped away to be with his Lord.

When your Christian loved ones come to bid you farewell in the hour of death or at the judgment, will it be "good night" or "good-bye"?

The Favorite Illustration of
W. E. DOWELL, Executive Vice Pres.
Baptist Bible College
Springfield, Missouri

UNLIMITED POTENTIAL IN THE SERVICE OF CHRIST

When I entered Baptist Bible College, Springfield, Missouri, I was a typical first-year student, searching for answers to questions. I was not settled on what I was going to do.

During that year something happened that was to change my life. I asked for a Sunday school class at the High Street Baptist Church and was given a little area with a curtain around it, a class book, and one eleven-year-old boy. I taught this boy for three or four weeks, until he finally brought a friend. I got so discouraged I went to the superintendent with the intention of giving up the class. He told me, "I didn't want to give you the class when you asked because my better judgment told me you were not serious and dedicated. I don't think you will make it in the ministry, but I went against my judgment and gave you the class." The middle-aged man finished, "I was right in my first judgment — you're worthless, so give me the book."

This made me so mad I told him I would not give him the book and I'd consider the class and pray about it. I went back to my room at the dormitory and began praying. I asked the dean of students for a key to an empty room on the third floor, and each afternoon for a week I went and prayed from half past one until five o'clock. God broke my heart over my failure with the small Sunday school class. I realized if I wasn't going to be faithful in little things, God would never bless me in big things. I prayed for the first boy and his family, and the boy he had brought and his family. Next I prayed for myself and my own needs, asking God to lead me to the right place.

God blessed the class, and new kids came. I prayed for them and their friends. On Saturday I cut a swath across every playground and empty lot I could find, seeking eleven-year-old boys. I would gather the class members and then go looking for their buddies and friends — for anyone who was eleven years old. When I left school in May of that year the Lord had given me fifty-six eleven-year-old boys for my class. All had been saved and many of their mothers, dads, and friends had also been saved. I realized for the first time that if I would pray and work, there was unlimited potential in the service of Christ.

The Favorite Illustration of
JERRY FALWELL, Pastor
Thomas Road Baptist Church
Lynchburg, Virginia

REDEEMED AND RELEASED

Dr. A. J. Gordon was pastor of a church in Boston many years ago. One day he met a little boy out in front of the church. The boy was carrying a rusty bird cage in his hands and several little birds were fluttering around on the bottom of the cage, as if they knew they were going to be destroyed. Dr. Gordon said, "Son, where did you get those birds?" The boy answered, "I trapped them out in the field." "What are you going to do with them?" the preacher asked. "I'm going to take them home and play with them and have some fun with them." "What will you do with them when you get through playing with them?" Dr. Gordon asked. "Oh," said the boy, "I guess I'll just feed them to an old cat we have around the house." Then Dr. Gordon asked the boy how much he would take for the birds and the boy answered, "Mister, you don't want these birds. They're just little old field birds and they can't sing very well." Dr. Gordon said, "I'll give you two dollars for the cage and the birds." "All right," said the boy, "it's a deal, but you're making a bad bargain." The exchange was made and the boy went whistling down the street, happy because he had two dollars in his pocket. Dr. Gordon took the cage out behind his church and opened the door of the cage and the birds flew out and went soaring away into the blue, singing as they went.

The next Sunday Dr. Gordon took the empty bird cage to the pulpit to use it in illustrating his sermon. He told his congregation all about the little boy and what had happened to the birds. Then he said, "That little boy said that the birds could not sing very well, but when I released them from the cage they went singing away into the blue, and it seems that they were singing, 'Redeemed, redeemed, redeemed.'"

Oh, my friends, you and I were like those little birds. Satan had us in the cage of sin and was taking us to hell. Then Jesus went to the cross and paid the price for our release and our redemption. Now when we come to Him in simple faith, we, too, can sing, "Redeemed, redeemed, I've been redeemed."

The Favorite Illustration of
HERSCHEL FORD, Author and Pastor
San Jose Baptist Church
Jacksonville, Florida

THE LONELY CABIN ON THE FORTY MILE

This is a true story, told by the principal character in it.

The story opens in Iowa with an old farmer by the name of J. Conlee. He was the father of twelve children, six boys and six girls, who grew up with every promise of becoming splendid citizens.

Some of the children had grown to manhood. One of the sons had become a lawyer and another a doctor. Still another was a professor in one of the seminaries. When the babe, about whom we speak, arrived, the father and mother did what they had done with every other child — they dedicated him to the Lord. In his boyhood days the mother said, "I hope my little Joe will be a preacher of the Gospel like two of his brothers are."

The years rolled by and Joe was a good boy and a credit to the home. One day when high school days were over the father said, "Joe, have you decided what you will be?"

"Yes, Father," said Joe, "the course I have taken in high school has fitted me for civil engineering. I think I will be a civil engineer."

A cloud came over his father's face as he said, "Oh, I am so sorry. We hoped you would enter the ministry. Are you sure you haven't heard the Lord's voice?"

He said he would pray about it. After two weeks he came to his father and said, "Father, my mind is made up. I will enter the ministry." His father embraced him and said he would send him to the University of Iowa.

When he had received his bachelor of arts degree he went for three years to the .... School at Ft. Dodge to fit himself for the ministry. One day one of the professors said to him, "You know there is a lot of superstition mixed up with what

44

we originally believed. You are a brilliant fellow. I heard the president say he considered you one of the most brilliant we have. Weigh everything carefully. Apply yourself to the study of books. I want you to read Darwin, Renan, and Huxley, every one of them philosophers."

When Joe Conlee came out of that school there was a battle of reason against faith — reason was winning in the great war.

He accepted the pastorate of a little Methodist Church in Iowa. There he married a splendid Christian girl, the daughter of a Methodist preacher in an adjoining town. After three years, because of his friendship with the bishop he was transferred to another Methodist church in California. He spent two years there. They gave him the honorary degree of doctor of divinity. And so he progressed in his ministerial aspirations.

But these were years in which he was fighting a tremendous battle with his soul. (Greater battles are fought within the confines of the human breast than were ever waged at historic Gettysburg, the Marne, or any other battlefield.) All the time he was drifting into Modernism, looking at the Scriptures from the Modernist's viewpoint. He was interpreting the Scriptures, not from the basis of faith, but from the basis of reason or intellectualism. He had been told that in order to be well balanced he should see both sides of the question, and should not be swayed by emotionalism in Methodism. The Methodist Conference met in Los Angeles and the bishop complimented him on his excellent work, and he was pastor of one of the largest Methodist churches on the Pacific coast.

After two years of successful ministry there he moved to a large church near Los Angeles. It was during this time that he built the lovely Methodist church of that place, a beautiful example of Spanish architecture. It was there that the seeds that had been sown in his heart in the past began to bear fruit. Joe confided to his wife that he was beginning to feel a little hypocritical — that he didn't believe the things his congregation demanded that he preach. He denied the virgin birth of Christ and the miracles. Finally he said, "I am going to quit. I cannot stand it."

One day Joe Conlee went into his pulpit and said, "My friends, I am about to make a confession. I cannot believe the Bible. There has been a battle in my heart for years. Now I feel I will regain some of my self-respect. This is the last time I will preach."

He was a gifted writer and soon got a job. He went to Santa Ana and became the editor of the *Santa Ana Herald*. For years his name was at the head of the editorial column. He began to smoke and drink, and gamble a little, then went from bad to worse.

He became president of the Free Thinkers Association of California. For twelve years he did not miss one night in the back room of the Mineral Saloon, giving lectures on atheism. He would raise his hand and defy God to strike him dead, and, when nothing happened, say, "You see, friends, there is no God." He would collect a few dimes and quarters and go into the saloon again to drink himself almost to death, to be carried off night after night to a praying wife. Delirium tremens seized him again and again. He became a hollow-eyed, emaciated, blaspheming, cursing, swearing, and carousing man. He had gone down into the very mud and scum of things — but every night his wife prayed for him.

Then came the great gold strike in Alaska. Men were climbing over the Chilkoot Pass on their way to the gold fields in a mad rush for the yellow metal. Conlee's friends thought if they could get him to change his environment, perhaps his life might be changed. The old drunk said he would be willing to go. So they packed his little trunk, bought him another suit of clothes and put him on the boat bound for Skagway.

His wife and little daughter came to see him off. His little girl Florence put her arms around his neck and said, "Daddy, dear Daddy, Mamma put in a little medicine chest that she thought you might need if you should get hurt there. And do not forget, Daddy, we will pray for you. And Daddy, inside the medicine chest I have put my little Book. I wouldn't give it to anybody else in the world but you, Daddy. You read it!"

That little Bible meant everything to Florence, and on the flyleaf she had written the words, "To my darling Daddy. With love from Florence. Do not forget, we love you." The whistle blew, and the old steamer plowed its watery way carrying Conlee and his trunk, and in the bottom of his trunk the little medicine chest with the Bible inside.

In a few weeks he was in that great seething, cursing, surging mass of humanity — prospectors arriving in the Yukon. The very first place he found was a saloon — the biggest in town. He got a job in that vile hell-hole.

One day the owner of a big place came to him and said, "Doc, I want you to go over to the 40-Mile. We have struck gold over there. I have bought the old log cabin and I want you to go out and hold the place."

"Not me," said Joe. "I will not leave here. You know my little weakness." He wasn't going where he couldn't get whiskey.

But the man said, "Joe, you can have all you want to drink. We will send supplies out for two weeks on the dog team. You'll have nothing to do but to sit in the cabin and have a wonderful time."

Joe Conlee found himself out in the lonely cabin on the 40-Mile, with nothing to do but drink. He had laid in a good supply, as winter was coming on and he wanted enough to last. The whiskey barrel was a quarter empty one day in October when there was a knock at the door of the cabin. There stood Jimmie Miller. He said he was cold and hungry. Jimmie Miller was Roman Catholic.

The latch-string is always out in Alaska. You dare not turn a man away. So Conlee said, "Come in, 'pard.' There's grub and a whiskey barrel." Jimmie Miller laughed as he entered the cabin door.

So the two of them sat down to drink. They were there two weeks, drinking themselves to sleep every night. The drunken orgies in that little cabin were beyond description. At the end of two weeks there came another knock at the door, and Wally Flett, a spiritualist medium from San Francisco came in. When he saw the liquor, his mouth watered, and he said, "Wouldn't you like me to stay with you?" They said, "Yes." There were three of them now in the cabin. Their ribald laughter, their filthy jesting, their obscene story-telling, their drinking and carousing were unspeakable.

November came . . . and went. They made three trips to Dawson with the dogs for whiskey and grub. The constant drinking got on their nerves; they cried and cringed in torment, with delirium tremens, night after night. Then for fun they had a spiritualistic seance; Wally Flett, the old medium, told how he used to bunco people. He showed them how the slate writing was done, and the tapping. Night after night that was the program for the three in the lonely cabin.

One night Jimmie Miller had delirium tremens and a high fever. In great agony he cried, "Get me a doctor. You can't let me lie here and die!" But they were forty miles from Dawson City. It was forty degrees below zero and the snows were deep. The delirious man kept screaming, "Get me a doctor!"

Then it was that Dr. Conlee remembered the medicine chest. He brought it out and when he opened it, out fell a little black Book on the floor. He opened the Book and read, "From Florence to Daddy" — Florence! Florence! "What you got, Conlee?" Wally Flett asked.

"It's a Bible, curse it!" and Conlee strode over to the stove.

As he lifted the lid to throw the Bible in, Wally Flett shouted, "Don't throw it in, man! Don't you know we haven't a thing to read in this God-forsaken country? Your only magazine I have read twenty times," and he snatched it from the hand of Joseph Conlee.

Dr. Conlee said, "If you want to read that you may, but I will not. . . . What was that written on the front page? 'To my darling Daddy. With love from Florence.'" He was a little more sober now. "My little girl! I am glad I didn't burn the Book my little Florrie gave me."

The medicine was effective and Jimmie Miller began to recover. As he was convalescing he started to read the Bible — aloud. Joe told him to shut up, but Wally Flett was interested. He said, "What was that you read, Jimmie?" Then Jimmie read it again.

Wally said, "I had no idea there were things like that in the Bible. What do you say if we read it just to pass the time away? — not to believe it. Joe was once a preacher; he tells us what fools preachers are."

So they took turns reading. Some days they would read five, six, even seven chapters. And gradually a change came into the lonely cabin on the 40-Mile. The whiskey barrel went down more slowly. When they came to the New Testament the cursings became fewer, the whiskey barrel began to be let alone entirely, and Wally Flett said, "Haven't you noticed a kind of change coming over us? I haven't heard swearing now for three or four days. I wonder if it's that Bible that's doing it?"

Christmas came. They read the story of the birth of Christ. Wally Flett said, "Wait a minute. Do you know what day it is? It's Christmas day. I wonder what the little kids are doing in the States? . . . What's the matter, Joe?"

"Oh, just thinking about little Florrie. She used to hang up a stocking every Christmas before I made such a fool of myself with the drink. There will be some happy folk around their firesides."

January came, and they started reading the Gospel of St. John. Then arrived the eventful day — February 14th. It was Wally's turn to read, and Joe got back of the stove: "Let not your heart be troubled. Ye believe in God, believe also in me. In my Father's house are many mansions: if it were not so I would have told you. I go to prepare a place for you."

Joe's hand brushed across his eyes.

"What's the matter, Joe?"

"Were you crying, Joe?"

"Yes, but go ahead; I am thinking about my little girl. I am not crying because of that Bible."

Then Wally said, "I'd like to know if this Book is true. For the last five days I've been wanting to pray, and I was scared you fellows would laugh at me, but I will not be scared any more. I shall ask God, if there be a God, to speak to me."

Joe said, "Well, since you have committed yourself, I will tell you that my heart has been broken for the last week. I can hear my mother back in Iowa praying — though she is now in heaven. What about you, Jimmie?"

"If you fellows want to pray, I'll pray with you."

Three old drunken soaks in the lonely cabin on the 40-Mile got down on their knees to pray. Their prayers rose higher and higher. Suddenly Wally Flett jumped to his feet, "Hallelujah! Hallelujah! Jesus heard me!" While he was shouting, up jumped Jimmie Miller; and then Joe Conlee arose shouting.

It was two o'clock in the morning when they arose from prayer. Into that lonely cabin on the 40-Mile had come the Man with the seamless robe. I can see Him standing in

Spirit by the old Yukon stove, as He put His hands on their heads.

Then Joe gets hold of the whiskey barrel and rolls it to the door. Wally goes for the hatchet and the cursed liquor runs out into the snow amid hilarious shouts of praise and thanksgiving to God. Surely the angels were looking over the battlements of heaven that night, watching the happenings in the lonely cabin on the 40-Mile. Jimmie Miller, Joe Conlee, and Wally Flett were born again by the Spirit of God!

Dr. Joseph Conlee became the dean of the Bible Standard School, and when this story was written both Wally Flett and Jimmie Miller were preaching the gospel. God had done a wonderful and permanent work in the lives of all three men. God can do the same for you! No matter how hard your case is — no matter how low you have fallen — no matter what your problem is — God is equal to it.

The Favorite Illustration of
DAVID OTIS FULLER, Pastor
Wealthy Street Baptist Church
Grand Rapids, Michigan

TEN THOUSAND MILES TO WIN A SOUL

I was living in New York City at the time, my mother and sister were still in Austria and father had already gone to Palestine to establish a home for us. When the news of my conversion reached my mother in Austria and my father in Jerusalem they were at first very reluctant to believe it, but when they finally had it in my own handwriting, it was like a bombshell to them. Mother and sister soon came to America with no other motive than to "rescue" me, while father at once considered me as one dead and spent seven days of mourning for me — a custom practiced by the Jews when a member of the family had died. Thenceforth, he would not permit my name to cross his lips.

Within the space of a brief article one cannot recount all that took place immediately following my conversion. I soon learned the meaning of the words, "If any man will come after me, let him deny himself, and take up his cross, and follow me," and "Think not that I am come to send peace on earth: I came not to send peace, but a sword. For I am come to set a man at variance against his father, and the daughter against her mother, and the daughter in law against her mother in law. And a man's foes shall be they of his own household. He that loveth father or mother more than me is not worthy of me: and he that loveth son or daughter more than me is not worthy of me. And he that taketh not his cross, and followeth after me, is not worthy of me" (Matt. 16:24; 10:34-38).

While a student at the Southern Baptist Theological Seminary in Louisville I had a surprise visit from my wealthy uncle and his wife. They offered me a fortune if I would give up my faith; and when I refused, it was they who sent for my mother and sister in Austria in the hopes that they could persuade me. Soon I had to make a choice between my own dear mother and my Saviour, which was enough to crush anyone. With broken hearts my mother and sister went to join Father in Jerusalem. My letters to them remained unanswered, for to them I was as one dead. When Mother passed away I was not even notified.

For a number of years I made many attempts to explain to Father the true meaning of my belief. I realized in what utter darkness he was concerning the true Christian faith. Humanly speaking it seemed that there could never be any reconciliation; however, I never stopped praying for him or writing to him.

Years passed. A gleam of hope appeared when a friend of mine, a Gentile believer who possessed an unbounded love of my people and who spoke the Hebrew language fluently and was thoroughly familiar with the traditions and beliefs of the Jews and mighty in the Scriptures, after several attempts managed to have a brief visit with father. He told him about me, assuring him that I had not departed from the faith of my fathers, that I still believed in the God of Abraham, Isaac, and Jacob. When he left he had father's promise that he would write me, and sure enough, around the Day of Atonement I received my first letter from Father urging me to repent and come "home." My faith was at once strengthened and I was determined as never before to go to Palestine and personally witness to him. That day finally came.

Arriving at the Lydda airport one morning I was met by

my sister-in-law who resided in Joppa. Though the daughter of a rabbi, she was quite tolerant and insisted on accompanying me to Jerusalem so as to lessen the shock to Father who had not seen me in twenty-five years, and to intercede in my behalf. It was eleven o'clock when we arrived in Jerusalem and I was told that Father was in the synagogue at prayer where he had been since five that morning, his daily custom. He would not partake of even a drop of water until he had finished his prayers. As I reached the door of the synagogue I spotted him, and in a few minutes I saw him remove his phylacteries. In all these years I had never had a picture of him; he simply refused to be photographed, saying that it was against the law of the Lord, which states: "Thou shalt not make unto thee any graven image, or any likeness of anything. . . . " I had my camera ready and standing aside I snapped several pictures of him as he came out of the synagogue. Then I walked up to him and placing my hands on his shoulders I asked whether he knew who I was. Speechlessly he looked at me. My sister-in-law then said, "Yes, this is your younger son Jacob." But it was still too much for him to grasp. For about five minutes more he stood there just looking at me. Then he began to feel me, first my hand, then my arms, then he moved his hands up to my head. Though he was almost totally blind and deaf, I saw the light of recognition light up those dimmed eyes and he repeated several times, "Mein sohn, mein sohn, Jankov fin America!" ("My son, my son, Jacob from America.") He simply could not believe that it was I! You can imagine the emotions that welled up within me.

We walked to his house and for several hours we talked without interruption. One of the first questions he asked me was whether I was living up to the teachings of the law and the traditions of the fathers. I replied that I believed in God's Word, every bit of which was precious to me. "Are you faithful in praying daily?" he asked, and I replied, "Not a day passes that I do not pray to the God of Abraham, Isaac, and Jacob." "Do you use the phylacteries and the prayer shawl?" (see Matt. 23:5) he asked. I had to answer No, and that was when a little argument ensued. I pointed out to him that in Deuteronomy 6:8 Moses did not mean for the Children of Israel to literally place a little case enclosing the

Scriptures on their forehead and another on the left arm near the heart for an hour or two during the morning prayers, but that his people should constantly have the law on their minds and hearts. My father argued that the wise men in Israel know better how to interpret the teachings of Moses than I.

When he went into another room to get a commentary on the Bible to point out to me what the holy rabbis have said, my sister-in-law pleaded with me to avoid entering into any such discussion as it might lead to unpleasantness. Yes, it would have been easy to drop the matter but within me a battle raged. Should I heed my sister-in-law's appeal and follow my own impulse to dismiss the subject and thus bring our visit to a pleasant climax? But then the Lord spoke to me.

Earnestly and lovingly I sought to show Father that every prophecy concerning the Messiah — the time of His coming, the place of His coming, the tribe from which He was to spring, and others — had been fulfilled. What puzzled him, as it has puzzled countless numbers of others like him, was how the Nazarene could be Israel's true Messiah when according to their beliefs (and traditions) the Messiah was not only to regather Israel to the Holy Land and reign over them, but to usher in universal peace according to Isaiah's prediction, "And they shall beat their swords into plowshares, and their spears into pruninghooks" (Isa. 2:4).

That afforded me a wonderful opportunity to explain to Father the Old Testament teaching of the two comings of the Messiah. He was to come first as the suffering servant, so clearly and convincingly predicted in Psalm 22, and Isaiah 53 which had already been fulfilled in Jesus of Nazareth. Then He was to come again to fulfill the rest of the prophecies as the reigning King who will usher in universal peace. I told Father that we today are privileged in that we are beginning to witness the fulfillment of this latter prediction.

I could see that it was the greatest revelation he had ever had. He lifted his hands and head and said, "I am waiting for Him." But in order to satisfy my own heart I asked, "Are you looking for Jeshua (Jesus)?" and he said, "Yes, Jeshua." I did not need any greater assurance of his faith. An inexpressible joy filled my heart and I felt that that one experience was well worth the journey of the more than ten thousand miles.

It was difficult to leave Father and when I bade him good-bye he grasped my hand and would not let me go. Finally I tore myself away from him and walked on. Before turning the corner I looked back and waved at him, and somehow I felt in my heart that it was the last time I would ever see him on this earth. And indeed it was, for not long afterward I received word that he had passed away. Like Simeon of old he had been waiting, hoping, and daily praying for the consolation of Israel, and having found Him he could say, "Lord, now lettest Thou Thy servant depart in peace, according to Thy Word, for mine eyes have seen Thy salvation."

> *The Favorite Illustration of*
> JACOB GARTENHAUS
> Founder and President
> International Board of Jewish Missions, Inc.
> Chattanooga, Tennessee

WE BURIED THE HATCHET THAT NIGHT

I had a good father, but I had almost driven him to the devil and hell with my terrible living. The first two weeks in August Mauldin Baptist Church had a two-week revival meeting. The speaker was Rev. Brown, a real live wire for God and a soul-winner if there ever was one. I thought it strange, but Dad went to the very first service of the revival. That night the minister delivered a wonderful, powerful sermon. I prayed earnestly that Dad would go to the prayer room, but he did not do so. I guess I must have been a little bit too anxious. At any rate, I went home disappointed. I prayed earnestly that night for my father; for I simply could not bear the thought of Dad's spending eternity in hell.

One morning about the middle of the first week of the meeting I was in my little study room praying for Dad, and the Lord said to me (in His still, small voice of the Spirit): "Son, you have never gone to your dad and told him that you are sorry for the way you have treated him, for stealing his money, and that you want him to forgive you for the heartaches you have caused him. . . ." That was true; for I had not asked Dad's forgiveness. The Lord had forgiven me, but I am sure my Dad had not done so, for I had caused him so much grief and sorrow.

I arose from my knees and began to look for my father. I found him sitting on the front porch in his favorite rocking chair. I went straight to him, sat down on the arm of the chair, put my arm around his neck, and said: "Dad, I want to tell you how sorry I am for the way I have treated you. I know that I have caused you many anxious hours and heartaches. I know that I have been a terribly bad boy, I know that I have caused you much trouble, and that I have stolen a lot of your money." By that time I was crying and the tears were dripping from my eyes onto Dad's trousers. Nevertheless, I continued as I ran my fingers through his grey hair, realizing that I myself had put many of them there, "Dad, I am responsible for many of these gray hairs in your head. . . . I'm sorry. I wish that I could live my life over, Dad. If I could, things would be different." I paused a moment . . . took a deep breath, reached into my pocket and pulled out the only ten-dollar bill I had in the world. . . . Then, holding it in my hand, I continued: "Dad, I stole a lot of your money; this you know very well. You know and I know that I could never repay all of it. My cotton was destroyed in the hailstorm along with yours. . . . I sold my hens and used that money to go to school. . . . I have no income now. . . . But I have this ten-dollar bill and I want to give it to you, Dad, as a payment on what I stole from you. . . ." I broke down and sobbed. I could not help it as I remembered the many times I had sneaked into Dad's room and taken money from his billfold. . . . I was hurting inside. . . . But when I raised my eyes there were two crying. . . . Dad's eyes were also filled with tears. This was the second time in my life that I had ever seen Dad cry. I laid the ten-dollar bill in his hand, tightened the arm I had around his neck, gave him a little hug, and got up and went back to my little room to thank God for the lifted burden — and also to claim Dad's soul for Jesus. I knew Dad was under conviction when I saw him break down and cry.

Just after dinner that day I went to my favorite place of prayer. It was a peach tree in the little peach orchard my father had on his farm. There was a peach in the orchard which made a perfect umbrella, and when the leaves were on the tree it completely hid me from the outside world. I loved to go there and pray. I went to that altar under the peach tree and prayed for God to save my father. That night at the revival God answered my prayer, and I saw Dad leave his seat and go to the prayer room for prayer.

The preacher delivered a powerful sermon that night on the "Judgment of God." I was praying while the preacher preached. I did not look up to see whether Dad had raised his hand for prayer, but on the first stanza of the invitation hymn Dad took Mother by the hand and walked down the aisle. The minister talked with them a few seconds, and then sent them on to the prayer room. Personal workers dealt with Dad and Mother (Mother had been saved, but was cold and indifferent); the victory was won.

Finally, I saw Dad come from the prayer room. He was still holding Mother's hand. He came straight to me, threw his arms around my neck and between broken sobs he said: "Son, we can be friends now. I now love you and we will get along all right." And at this our tears met! We buried the hatchet that night, and ever afterward Dad and I were real pals until he went home to be with Jesus. I did not know much about the rapture at that time, but I was happy enough that night to have been raptured!

Don't feel badly toward my father for hating me. If I had treated you as I treated him, you too would have hated me. I was the vilest, most unlovely, most unlovable, and most despicable rascal whom God ever let live!

That night Dad called all the children to his bedroom and got down on his old knees and prayed. One of the girls was saved at that first family altar in the Greene home. We had a reborn father and we also had a new home after that. Our home was so happy!

Shortly after my conversion I was introduced to the Scofield Bible by an old saint of God, a missionary returned from China. I shall never cease to praise God for that dear man. I do not know his name, but he advised me to get a Scofield Bible. This I did and I learned to love it. But I wanted my father also to have a Scofield Bible, so I got busy and did enough odd jobs to make $6.50 with which I bought Dad a Scofield Bible. He loved it from the beginning, and through the years he very nearly wore it out. He used it until he died. Dad lived for Jesus eleven years here on earth, and then Jesus called him home.

The Favorite Illustration of
OLIVER B. GREENE,
Evangelist and Director of the Gospel Hour
Greenville, South Carolina

THE PEACE OF GOD WAS THERE

"And the peace of God, which passeth all understanding, shall keep your hearts and minds through Christ Jesus" (Phil. 4:7).

"God controls the unexpected." That was the main emphasis behind my oral testimony given at the Wednesday prayer meeting of Grace Baptist Church. Two days later, on Friday afternoon, the unexpected happened. My family and I were on our way to a cafeteria. A drunk, on the opposite side of the grassy median, had just driven through a red light. Coming upon slow-moving traffic, he suddenly darted to the left, across the median, and on to the pavement in front of our car. A terrible crash followed. Did God control this unexpected event? He certainly did — a truth for which our family praises Him.

When I became conscious in the wreckage, a sense of total helplessness overwhelmed me. I could hear my children crying in the back seat, but I could do nothing. In fact, I heard my twelve-year-old son screaming, "My daddy is dead; my daddy is dead." I could hear my wife talking incoherently beside me, but I could not reach out toward her. Then an awareness of my own physical condition hit me. My chest was full of pain (caused by broken ribs and a severe lung contusion). My jaw felt broken. I wondered about my neck because it felt limp. I had never experienced such pain and helplessness before.

Then the peace and comfort of God just filled my soul, and I was buoyed up by an awareness of His presence. I realized that only God could cope with the situation. I prayed, "Lord, take care of my wife. Take care of my children. Into your hands I commit them and myself. Thy will be done."

All at once, those passages which I had read, heard, studied, and preached upon, were made real and personal through the internal witness of the Holy Spirit. The peace of God was just *there*. It was not drummed up; it was there! It was real! It passed all understanding! There was no panic — no frustration — no depression, only the quiet rest of the soul in the lap of God. It was a fantastic experience.

The Favorite Illustration of
ROBERT GROMACKI, Chairman
Division of Biblical Education
Cedarville College
Cedarville, Ohio

"HE SAID THAT HE WOULD COME BACK, AND I BELIEVED HIM"

The one Bible doctrine that keeps me going, even in times of great frustration and disappointment, is the hope of the second coming of Jesus Christ. I will always be indebted to a Southern Baptist preacher, B. B. Crim, who preached on the second coming of the Lord at a revival he held in my home town of Texarkana, Texas, when I was a boy of thirteen. Since then, I have refused to let the burdens of life get me down. Even as we face the sobering successes of international communism and realize the extent of the communist revolution within the United States, we still have faith and hope as we reflect upon the second coming of Jesus Christ . . . the rapture of the church and the home-going of the believers.

When I was a boy, I heard an illustration which I have never forgotten. It seems that a young girl of eleven or twelve was swimming off the beach at Long Beach, California, with her father. She was a good swimmer, in spite of her tender age. Because she was an only child, her father was especially fond of her and was thrilled that he could go swimming with the one dearest on earth to him. It was a beautiful balmy day, and the father soon realized that he and his daughter had swum too far from shore. Looking back, the Long Beach public beach was like a speck on the horizon. The father grew panicky, but the child did not. Successfully hiding his concern, the father said, "We swam out too far. Daddy is too tired to get you back. Would you mind floating out here until I swim back and get help?" The little girl said, "No." She didn't mind waiting for her father's return. After awhile, the father came back in a rescue boat. The little girl was safe and sound, floating in the water. After she was brought to shore, a newspaper man heard of the courageous little eleven-year-old, floating alone far out in the ocean. He rushed up to the little girl and said, "Weren't you afraid? I bet you were scared to death. Tell me, weren't you afraid?" To which the little girl replied, "No, I wasn't afraid. You see, that man standing over there is my daddy. He said that he would come back, and I believed him."

My Heavenly Father and His only begotten Son, Jesus Christ, have promised to come back for me. As I wait in a world filled with anxieties and faithlessness and war and turmoil, I keep floating with full assurance that Jesus will someday come back and rescue His own. We dare not be over-anxious about the problems of this life. After all, He has promised to come back, and He will.

The Favorite Illustration of
BILLY JAMES HARGIS
Founder-Director
Christian Crusade
Tulsa, Oklahoma

REAL LOVE

The nurse wheeled nine-year-old Jimmy into the hospital ward. Jimmy's little sister, Susan, was desperately ill with a rare blood disease. The only hope for her was to success-fully transfuse several pints of blood into her frail little body.

When they asked Jimmy if he'd be willing to help his sister live by giving her some of his blood, he replied, "Of course." And so the doctors readied the instruments for the delicate transfusion of blood. When they inserted the tube into his arm, Jimmy looked up from the hospital bed. "Doctor," he asked with a pale smile, "When will I die?"

Imagine that! Jimmy thought helping his sister get well meant he would have to give his life — and yet he said, "Of course." That, believe me, is real love.

The Favorite Illustration of
GUNNAR HOGLUND, Pastor
Emmanuel Baptist Church
Santa Clara, California

CHRIST, THE BRIDGE BETWEEN DARKNESS AND LIGHT

It is affirmed in Holy Writ that Christ "humbled himself" and became obedient unto death (Phil 2:8).

Most people are agreed that humbling one's self means to become lower than he is, but no one is quite sure just how low this actually is. In this verse the word *humbled* helps to explain the act. The Greek work in the original comes from a root which means "carpet," or that which is level with the ground. It is low enough to be walked upon, or used. Christ did this when He humbled Himself and became obedient unto death. He formed a bridge spanning the chasm between the kingdom of darkness and the kingdom of light, and all saved men have walked over that bridge into the kingdom of light.

During the great Reformation in Europe, Luther and Zwingli found themselves at odds in their concern for the movements they were leading. Early one morning, Zwingli walked out on the mountains of Switzerland and a soul-stirring sight confronted him. He saw two goats making their way over a narrow path on the mountain. One was ascending the trail, the other descending. He also noticed that they must pass at a point where the trail was so narrow that there was room for only one goat. He watched to see what would happen. The animals rounded a turn in the path which brought them in full view of each other. They backed up, as though ready for a lunge, and then the most amazing thing happened. The goat on the trail below laid down in the path, while the goat above him walked over his back. The first animal then arose and continued his journey up the trail. To Zwingli this meant that the way down is the way up, which is the course that Christ took. He humbled Himself so that men could walk over Him into the kingdom of light, knowing that afterward He would be exalted.

The Favorite Illustration of
HERMAN A. HOYT, President
Grace Theological Seminary
Winona Lake, Indiana

THERE IS A LIVING GOD WHO LEADS HIS PREACHERS

As a young preacher I was invited to preach a youth revival in a southwestern city. It was a very wealthy, large, and fashionable church. The first Sunday evening I was told by the pastor, who was in his seventies, that the church tolerated no loud preaching and certainly no emotion. Being in my early twenties I was apprehensive and yes, a little bit scared. I preached on Sunday night and there were no visible results. The same thing was true on Tuesday night and Wednesday night. In every way the meetings appeared to be complete failures. Wednesday night I went to my room and resolved to pray all night for God's power and blessing. About five o'clock in the morning the dear Lord seemed to assure me that the victory would come that evening. I rejoiced in this assurance and believed that God had spoken to me. When the time for the evening service arrived I had decided to speak on the prodigal son. Now when I speak on the prodigal son I call the characters by name. The prodigal son is named Bill and his brother is named John. I act the story out. I began talking about the early events of the parable and got to the place or point of naming the prodigal son, but to save me I could not think of the name *Bill*. I backed off and started over again. When I got to the naming of the prodigal son, again the name *Bill* escaped me. The third time I tried. Again and again I tried. Finally I called the prodigal son by his brother's name, John, thinking by the time I got to the brother I could give him the name of the prodigal son, but still I couldn't think of *Bill*. I had already given Bill John's name and I was trying to think of Bill so I could give that name to John. I backed up and tried again but still could not think of the name *Bill*. Again and again I tried and failed. Finally in desperation I said, "The brother didn't have a name. They called him Little Bud for short." So there I was calling Bill John and John Little Bud. Did I ever get confused! The sermon seemed to be in every way a failure; in fact some folks, realizing my predicament, were snickering.

When I finished the sermon I could hardly wait to get out of the auditorium and away from my embarrassment. During the invitation, however, a young man back in the back on my left started toward the aisle. To be quite frank, I was surprised that anyone would come to the aisle after my message. When he arrived at the aisle, however, he turned and went toward the back door. Again, to be frank, I could hardly blame the fellow for walking out. However, when he got to the back row he stopped and put his arm around a lady, and she began to praise the Lord. Then the two of them ran down the aisle and threw themselves in the altar. Seeing this the chairman of the deacon board who was sitting in the front row jumped in the altar and began praising God with them. Soon the pastor who had told me that no emotion was allowed was on his knees in the altar joining in the praise. The choir began to weep and could not sing. The music director could not see to lead the singing. Numbers of other people joined the happy altar scene and real revival broke out. I had no idea what had happened, but I knew I liked it.

Finally the pastor gained enough composure to ask me to lead the closing prayer. After which I walked toward the side door. Just as I arrived at the door the church secretary took me by the shoulder and turned me around. With tears and emotion she asked, "Who told you?" I replied, "Who told me what?" She said, "Who told you to preach on the prodigal son? You see, the young man who came forward tonight was the son of the deacon chairman. He was a prodigal son who ran away from home one year ago. He is now twenty. No one knew he was within a thousand miles of this place tonight. We were all stunned to see him in the service as we walked in. Then when you announced that you were preaching on the prodigal son, we knew you must have been told of his presence. He came home tonight, got saved, and is going back to his parents. That is what happened in the altar tonight."

I felt praise swelling in my own heart and turned to walk out the door.

The church secretary then asked, "But who told you his name was John?"

I could hardly believe my ears. 'Twas the Holy Spirit who kept me from remembering the prodigal son's name. It was the Holy Spirit who led me to call the prodigal son *John* instead of *Bill*.

The church secretary had still another question. "Who told you he has a brother whose nickname is Little Bud?"

By that time I was about to shout! 'Twas the Holy Spirit who would not let me think of the name *Bill* and who led me to call the prodigal son *John* and his brother *Little Bud*.

This young preacher went to his room that night and stayed on his knees most of the night in praise, prayer, and thanksgiving that there is a living God who leads His preachers who pay the price of waiting on Him.

The Favorite Illustration of
Jack Hyles, Pastor
First Baptist Church
Hammond, Indiana

YOU CAN BE SURE OF SALVATION

During my ministry as a pastor for more than fourteen years, and as an evangelist for more than eight years, I have found very few people who know they are saved. Some of them *think so*, and others *hope so,* but not many really *know so*. Consequently, one of my favorite messages which I preach in evangelism is entitled "Three Things You Can Be Sure of."

The first point is: You can be sure of the *Scriptures*: "The law of the Lord is perfect, converting the soul: the testimony of the Lord is *sure,* making wise the simple" (Ps. 19:7).

The second point is: You can be sure of *sin*: ". . . be sure your *sin* will find you out" (Num. 32:23).

The third point is: You can be sure of *salvation*: "Wherefore the rather, brethren, give diligence to make your calling and election *sure . . ."* (II Peter 1:10). I often use this illustration told by J. Wilbur Chapman, a well-known evangelist of years ago, to close the message:

I will tell you how to be saved, and how you may know you are a Christian. I was studying for the ministry, and I heard that D. L. Moody was to preach in Chicago, and I went down to hear him. I finally got into his after meeting, and I shall never forget the thrill that went through me, when he came and sat down beside me, an inquirer. He asked me if I was a Christian. I said, "Mr. Moody, I am not sure whether I am a Christian or not."

He asked whether I was a church member, and I said I was, but was not always sure whether I was a Christian or not. He very kindly took his Bible and opened it at the fifth chapter of John, the twenty-fourth verse, which reads as follows: "Verily, verily, I say unto you, He that heareth my word and believeth on him that sent me *hath* everlasting life and shall not come into condemnation; but is passed from death unto life."

Suppose you had read that for the first time, wouldn't you think it was wonderful? I read it through, and he said: "Do you believe it?" I said, "Yes." "Do you accept it?" I said, "Yes." "Well, are you a Christian?" "Mr. Moody, I sometimes think I am, and sometimes I am afraid I am not."

He very kindly said, "Read it again."

So I read it again. "Verily, verily, I say unto you, He that heareth my word and believeth on him that sent me hath everlasting life, and shall not come into condemnation, but *is passed* from death unto life."

Then he said, "Do you believe it?" I said, "Yes." "Do you receive *Him?*" I said, "Yes." "Well," he said, "are you a Christian?"

I just started to say over again that sometimes I was afraid I was not, when, the only time in all the years I knew him and loved him, he was sharp with me. He turned on me with his eyes flashing and said, "See here, whom are you doubting?"

Then I saw it for the first time, that when I was afraid I was not a Christian I was doubting God's Word. I read it again with my eyes overflowing with tears.

Since that day I have had many sorrows and many joys, but never have I doubted for a moment that I was a Christian, because God said it.

Now what I ask you to do is to plant your feet upon this promise, and say, "Yes, from this moment I know I am a Christian."

The Favorite Illustration of
CARL JOHNSON, Evangelist
Beckley, West Virginia

"I DON'T HAVE A LEG TO STAND ON"

A few years ago during a meeting in Norfolk, Virginia, a chaplain in the United States Navy stood and gave the following testimony:

When I finished high school I was religious but not a Christian. When I finished college I was religious, but not a Christian. I got a degree from seminary, but, though I was preparing for the ministry, I had not truly become a Christian. I was ordained to a gospel ministry and bore the name *Christian,* but was not truly converted. I was commissioned as an officer and a chaplain in the United States Navy, but had never been born-again. While in charge of military prisoners in the State of Washington a convict came to me and asked me to start a Bible class among the prisoners. I put him off with some excuse, but over and over he came back. Finally, I said, "I'll be ready for him the next time," and then when he came, I said, "You start the class and you be the teacher." I thought, "that will hold him," but to my surprise he said, "Sir, I have never been beyond the sixth grade, but I'll do the best I can." I had to attend the class since I was responsible for what happened. From the very first day when the convict, who had never gone beyond the sixth grade, stood there and read from his big thick Bible and dropped his tears on its leaves while telling of his recent conversion from a life of awful sin, I found no peace until I had found the Saviour of this convict. I tried to get rid of my feeling that I was wrong and that he was right, but I could not laugh it off, think it off, or in any other way get rid of the feeling that I needed, and must have, what that man had.

One day, while walking down the streets of San Francisco, I saw a man rolling himself along on a little wagon made of skate wheels. The man had no legs, and was strapped to the wagon, but he was able to make rapid progress by pushing himself along with his hands. We both came to the intersection about the same time. He rolled out to the street car track, came perilously close to the tracks, and stopped. I wondered how he would get aboard the street car, and waited to see. The car rolled up, stopped, and the doors opened. The man on the wagon smiled and threw his hands above his head. A kindly conductor smiled, reached down, and lifted him in. There on the street I staggered in my sins and cried out to God, "There I am, Lord. I don't have a leg to stand on." I, at last, threw my arms up to God as a helpless sinner, not trying to stand on my education, ordination, or commission, or anything else in this world. The great Conductor of the universe lifted me in.

I have seen this young officer many times since the war. I have seen his testimony which has been put into print. The last time I saw him he had brought some forty young people to a Bible conference where I was a speaker. He told me that he was planning to go to Japan as a missionary.

The Favorite Illustration of
Jimmy Johnson, Evangelist
Fuquay-Varina, North Carolina

ONCE YOUR SAVIOUR, NOW YOUR JUDGE

A young fellow in his early teens was riding a horse down one of the side streets of a small midwestern town when the horse started on a runaway gallop. The inexperienced lad could not control the horse and panicked as the animal headed for a cluster of big trees. He knew his life was in danger and screamed for help. A young lawyer heard his cry, saw the situation, and grabbed the reins; finally, holding the horse, he waited for the young man to quickly dismount.

"You saved my life," said the lad in sincere apprecation. "Thank you very much."

Years later in a court of justice, a middle-aged man stood before a jury and a judge, accused of murder. The jury found him guilty. The judge called him to the bench and asked if he had anything to say before he pronounced sentence.

"Remember me?" said the prisoner.

"Yes I do," replied the judge.

"I am the teen-ager you saved several years ago in my hometown" the man continued. "Remember the runaway horse . . . you saved my life, your Honor. Please do it again today."

"When I saved you from the horse, I was your savior," said the young lawyer of years ago. "Today I am your judge, passing sentence on what you have done which is punishable by law. I have no other choice."

Someday we will stand before the Judge of all nations. What will His decision be? It will be based on what we have done with Jesus who is the Saviour of the world. Let Christ be your Saviour *now*. Those who reject Him give the Judge only one possible choice.

The Favorite Illustration of
MEL JOHNSON, Director
Tips for Teens
Roseville, Minnesota

GOD'S FIDDLE

Many years ago when Bob Jones University was still Bob Jones College and we had three or four hundred students, a young lady came into my office one day. She was a freshman, and had just returned from taking her music lesson. She put down her violin and her music books and said, "Dr.

Bob, I want to talk to you. I do not have the joy I ought to have as a Christian. I wonder if you could help me find the trouble." Now, frankly, I was amazed. The school was small enough in those days so that I got pretty well acquainted with every student; and if I had been asked to name two or three of the most spiritual girls in the freshman class, I would have named Dorothy as one. I said, "Dorothy, is there any sin in your life?" She said, "No, Dr. Bob, not if I know my heart." I said, "Are you holding back anything from God?" She said, "No. Do you remember what I wrote you when I applied for admission last summer?" I remembered. She had written something like this from her home in North Carolina. "Dear Dr. Jones: I was saved last week in a meeting one of your preacher boys held in my home church. I have been playing in a dance band. Now I have given my violin to the Lord, and I want to play it for Him. I want to come to Bob Jones College because I know you have a Christian student body and a godly faculty, and I know you have a good music department. I want to be the best possible musician for Christ. My family is unsaved and does not want me to go. They say I can stay here in town and go to a state school. It is going to mean a complete break with my family, but I believe the Lord wants me there."

Dorthy had been in school about three months the day she sat in my office. I said, "You are not holding anything back?" She said, "No, I have not had a letter from my family since I left home." "What about the fiddle?" I said. She said, "Don't you know I told you I was going to play it just for the Lord? It is the Lord's now." I said, "That is fine, Dorothy. This is God's violin. You are going to play it for Him. Suppose God tells you to keep your fingers off His fiddle? How about that?" She said, "You mean not play?" I said, "Yes, I mean never play another note." She said, "Dr. Bob, you don't think God wants me to give up my music, do you?" "I don't think so, Dorothy. God gives us talent to be trained and used and invested; but it may be He wants you to lay this 'idol' on the altar. It may be He knows you love music too much; it may be that music is taking His place. Suppose it is more for His glory for this instrument to be mute than to be breathing out melody? How about that, Dorothy?" She began to cry. She said, "Dr. Bob, I could not live without my violin. I will use it for the Lord, but I just couldn't give it up!" I said, "Dorothy, I think we have found your trouble."

I watched Dorothy the next day at chapel. When you stand on the platform and watch the students sing, when they are at their best, it is like looking into the sun at noonday; but Dorothy that day was like looking at a cloud in an otherwise cloudless sky — miserable and unhappy. I watched her, and I prayed for her. The next day and the next she looked that way; but the following day I could hardly see her face for her mouth — she was smiling all the way across. I thought, "She has settled it." Later that day she came into my office with her violin and put it on my desk. She said, "Dr. Bob, I want you to see God's fiddle. If He wants me to play it, I will play it for His glory; but if He says, 'Don't touch it again; do not ever play another note,' that is all right, too. I love Him more than I love music or anything else."

That is what it means to forsake all and follow Him. That is the test of our love for Christ — to have no plans except the plans of His making, no friends except the friends of His choosing, no husband, no wife except the husband, or wife, of His ordaining, no will except the will to do His will. "He that doeth the will of God abideth forever."

The Favorite Illustration of
BOB JONES, Chancellor
Bob Jones University
Greenville, South Carolina

GOD IS ABLE

A great many people have asked me to explain *how* God will raise the dead. In Philippians 3:21 Paul tells us that we are to look for the Lord from heaven "Who shall change our vile body, that it may be fashioned like unto his glorious body, according to the working whereby he is able. . . ." If anyone has a doubt as to whether the Lord Jesus Christ can take our vile bodies and make them look like His own glorious body, I would like to settle that doubt now.

In Gary, Indiana, there is probably the largest steel mill of any place in the world. Running through those mills are hard, dirty, black beaten paths which the employees travel as they go about their work. These paths are composed of four elements — clay, sand, soot, and moisture.

Now, let's take this path an element at a time and hand it up to the Son of God and let Him work upon it according to the mighty working of His power whereby He is able.

We hand the clay up to Him and He submits it to such heat and pressure that in the fullness of time He hands it back to us in a hard crystalline form that reflects the blue rays of the sun and rejects all others. We call it a sapphire.

We now hand the sand up to Him and let Him work upon it according to the mighty working of His power. He submits it to heat and pressure and in the fullness of time hands it back to us a hard, crystalline substance. We call it an opal.

We come now to the black soot. Before we hand it up to the Son of God to see what He can do with it, let us remind ourselves that it is the unburned carbon that has been belching out of the chimneys through the years. He takes this black carbon, submits it to heat and pressures, and in the fullness of time hands it back to us the hardest and whitest substance known. We call it a diamond.

We now come to the path and take the remaining element — the moisture — the water. We hand that up to the Son of God and let Him work upon it according to the mighty working of His power and He distills it into a dewdrop. It hangs on the leaf of the rosebush and in its beauty outshines the sapphire, the opal, and the diamond.

If Jesus Christ can transform the pathway in an old Gary steel mill into sapphires, opals, diamonds, and dewdrops, I have no doubt as to what He can do with this two-hundred-pound body of mine when He raises it from the dust of the grave or from the sidewalk and makes it look like His own glorious body.

The Favorite Illustration of
ROBERT T. KETCHAM,
Author and Conference Speaker
Chicago, Illinois

EACH GIVES WHAT HE HAS

East Berlin is communist controlled.

West Berlin is free.

Some people in East Berlin one day took a truckload of garbage and dumped it on the West Berlin side.

The people of West Berlin could have done the same thing. But instead they took a truckload of canned goods, bread, and milk . . . and neatly stacked it on the East Berlin side.

On top of this stack they placed the sign:

EACH GIVES WHAT HE HAS.

The Favorite Illustration of
SALEM KIRBAN, Author
Huntingdon Valley, Pennsylvania

THE WRONG WEAPONS

Clarence Hall, a World War II correspondent, gave this remarkable testimony:

"I can never think of the boons and benefits that the Bible invariably brings without thinking of Shimmabuke, a tiny village I came upon as a war correspondent in Okinawa.

"Thirty years before, an American missionary en route to Japan had stopped there just long enough to make two converts — Shosei Kina and his brother Mojon. He left a Bible with them and passed on. For thirty years they had no contact with any other Christian missionary, but they made the Bible come alive! They taught the other villagers until every man, woman, and child in Shimmabuke became a Christian.

"Shosei Kina became the headman of the village, and Mojon the chief teacher. In the school the Bible was read daily. The precepts of the Bible were law in the village. In those thirty years there developed a Christian democracy in its purest form.

"When the American army came across the island, an advance patrol swept up to the village compound with guns leveled. The two old men stepped forth, bowed low, and began to speak. An interpreter explained that the old men were welcoming the Americans as fellow Christians!

"The flabbergasted GIs sent for their chaplain. He came with officers of the Intelligence Service. They toured the village. They were astounded at the spotlessly clean homes and streets and the gentility of the inhabitants. The other Okinawan villages they had seen were filthy, and the people were ignorant and poverty-stricken.

"Later I strolled through Shimmabuke with a tough army sergeant. He said, 'I can't figure it out — this kind of people coming from a Bible and a couple of old guys who wanted to live like Jesus Christ. Maybe we have been using the wrong kind of weapons to make the world over!' "

The Favorite Illustration of
WALTER B. KNIGHT,
Minister to Shut-ins and the Sick
Austin, Texas

"BUT I WANT TO BE SAVED"

While a pastor in Milwaukee, Wisconsin, I received a letter from a lady in Michigan requesting me to make a call on a dying man. Neither the writer of the letter nor the man upon whom she wished me to call were known to me. She stated, moreover, that she had no idea how I would be received. These are not the easiest calls for a pastor to make!

The wife of the dying man responded to the ringing of the doorbell. I identified myself and told her the reason for my making this call, namely, a letter from a friend of hers in Michigan. It was a cold, winter afternoon and the attitude of the wife was almost as chilling. After a few moments, however, she invited me in and directed me to the sick room where her husband lay in great pain.

As I approached his bed I sought to speak with him but

detected that he was suffering greatly. I stayed only a few minutes with the promise that I would return in just a few days, to which he replied, "I hope you will come back." After praying at his bedside I turned to the wife and said, "I will return in just a few days." She said, "You heard what my husband said — that he wants you to come back." With this I left.

After three or four days I returned and was again met at the door by the wife whose greeting was more cordial than on my first visit. Her reply to my inquiry regarding her husband was, "Yes, you may come and see him but he will not understand a word you will say, as he is in a coma." My heart sank as I realized that here was a man going out into eternity without Christ — a lost sinner! Standing at his bedside I spoke to him but received as response only the groans of a dying man. As his wife stood in the doorway of the bedroom, I said, "Well, we will pray together."

I leaned over near to the ear of the dying man. In my prayer I made the way of salvation just as clear as possible, trusting that although he could not respond to me, that the heart of this dying man would yet be opened to the Saviour. The prayer concluded, I was about to turn and leave the room, when in a strong voice he made the following appeal, "But I want to be saved!" I returned to his bedside and there had the great privilege of pointing this man to the Saviour of sinners. Although he had made no response earlier in the visit, yet at this time he was able to pray and make known to Christ the fact that he was a sinner and was now receiving Him as his Saviour. How gracious of God not only to have saved this dying sinner but also in giving one of His servants a second opportunity, after what had been an initial failure, to win this lost man.

The Favorite Illustration of
WILLIAM E. KUHNLE
Assistant to the National Representative
General Association of Regular Baptists

THE YOUNG MAN DEFEATED THE DEVIL

My friend, Dr. Bartholow, of Mount Vernon, New York, in his address on "The Philosopher's Stone" tells this:

In my youth I was taught the game of chess. For many years I have studied the game and know that it is a game of exhaustless moves. More than a million moves have been analyzed. Steinitz, Tarrasch, Philsbury, Larker, Capablanca, Alexhine, have made valuable contributions to the study of chess in our day, and the end is not yet.

All who know the game know that the checkmating of the king is the objective of the contestants. The great variety of pieces, with their multiplicity of movement in combination, makes for profundity and variety in the play. One adept at chess is able ofttimes to announce a checkmate of an opponent's king in a certain number of moves. Obviously, this requires a close and comprehensive knowledge of all the moves possible by the various pieces under all conditions. Should a player announce a checkmate in four moves, it would mean that his opponent had no possible way of escape, no matter what combination he should form with his own pieces.

Years ago, from a great chess player of Cincinnati, we learn that in the early part of the last century an artist who was also a great chess player painted a picture of a chess game. The players were a young man and Satan. The young man manipulated the white pieces, Satan the black pieces. The issue of the game was this: should the young man win, he was to be forever free from the power of evil; should the devil win, the young man was to be his slave forever. The artist evidently believed in the supreme power of evil, for his picture presented the devil as victor.

In the conception of the artist, the devil had just moved his queen and had announced a checkmate in four moves. The young man's hand hovered over his rook; his face paled with amazement — there was no hope. The devil wins! He was to be a slave forever.

For years, this picture hung in a great art gallery. Chess players from all over the world viewed the picture. They acquiesced in the thought of the artist. The devil wins! After several years a chess doubter arose; he studied the picture and became convinced that there was but one chess player upon the earth who could give him assurance that the artist of this picture was right in his conception of the winner. The chess player was the aged Paul Morphy, a resident of New Orleans, Louisiana. Morphy was a supreme master of chess in his day, an undefeated champion. He had quit the game because of mental strain. A scheme was arranged by our chess doubter through which Morphy was brought to Cincinnati to view the chess picture.

On beholding the picture, two mighty impulses arose in the old master's mind: the first, that which leads a brave man to take the part of the under dog; the second, that which resents the passing of a crown of supremacy which had not been challenged.

Morphy stood before the picture, five minutes, ten minutes, twenty minutes, thirty minutes. He was all concentration; he lifted and lowered his hands as, in imagination, he made and eliminated moves. Suddenly, his hand paused, his eyes burned with the vision of an unthought-of-combination. Suddenly, he shouted, "Young man, make that move. That's the move!"

To the amazement of all, the old master, the *supreme chess personality,* had discovered a combination that the creating artist had not considered. The young man defeated the devil. The *master* personality had come!

The Favorite Illustration of
ROBERT G. LEE, Pastor Emeritus
Bellevue Baptist Church
Memphis, Tennessee

THE RUNAWAY SALESMAN

Steward Webber, a young and "successful" salesman, left his wife and daughter and spent New Year's Day, 1939, in an Ashland, Ohio, saloon.

Drink, riotous living, and a crushing gambling debt of ten thousand dollars (half of which he had stolen from his company) drove him to despair and thoughts of suicide.

That night, miserable, alone, without hope and afraid, he opened the hotel window . . . but he didn't jump!

For at that very moment, he learned later, his brother Leland was on his knees praying for his wayward brother.

The next morning Steward left Ashland. He didn't know where he was going — just anywhere to get away from it all.

Nearing Indianapolis he thought, "I'll stop and tell that radio preacher to keep preaching — he might save others from my fate."

The minister led him to Christ! Steward became a "new creature in Christ" (II Cor. 5:17). He walked out a new man, *free* from the guilt condemnation of his sins, and delivered from drink and rotten living.

Though the preacher urged him to go home, he decided to remain in town for awhile.

The next morning on the radio the speaker told about the young runaway salesman from Ohio, and how he had been saved. He urged the wife, if she was listening, to take him back.

His brother heard the broadcast. "That's Steward!" he cried.

A few days later as Steward walked past the Indianapolis post office he had a strange urge to go in and inquire if there was mail there for him.

Ridiculous! No one knew where he was. How could there be mail there for him? But sure enough, there *was* a letter — from his wife! " . . . if that was you the preacher told about, Steward, come home!"

Great! Out on the highway he picked up the first hitch-hiker and witnessed to him so earnestly that the poor man begged, "Let me out of here!" — in pouring rain!

Back in Ashland he confessed his sins. The judge gave him a suspended two- to ten-year prison sentence. Needless to say he lost everything — house, furnishings, and all.

The Webbers moved to Anderson, Indiana. God blessed Steward with a good job. In less than four years he had paid back all he had owed.

He took the last payment back to Ashland and delivered it personally, that he might witness of God's grace.

He went to the judge and said, "I have paid my debt. Now I want to clear up anything else that is against me."

"Mr. Webber," he said, "there is no charge here against you. The record is clear."

God Almighty, the great Judge of the universe had also cleared the record against Steward Webber!

"Being justified freely by *his* grace through the redemption that is in Christ Jesus" (Rom. 3:24). "There is therefore now no condemnation to them that are in Christ Jesus" (Rom. 8:1). "He that believeth on Him is not condemned" (John 3:18).

In 1948 Mr. Webber founded the Belmont Bible Church in Anderson, Indiana, where he is pastor and where it has been my privilege to conduct meetings.

The Favorite Illustration of
PAUL J. LEVIN, Evangelist
Waterloo, Iowa

WHATEVER IS IN COMES OUT

Two jars which stood on a table looked alike, but their contents were different. When one was turned on its side, honey ran out. When the other was turned on its side, vinegar ran out.

Why did vinegar come out of the one? Because it was upset. But the other was also upset, and no vinegar came out of it. Of course; it had no vinegar in it.

The explanation is that when a jar is upset, whatever is in it comes out. Until the jars were upset, they looked alike. The difference lay within, and could not be seen. When they were upset, their contents were revealed.

Often until we are upset we put on a good front. But when we are upset, we reveal our inner thoughts and attitudes. " . . . [out] of the abundance of the heart his mouth speaketh" (Luke 6:45). Frequently it is our *reactions* rather than our premeditated actions which reveal our true attitudes.

The Favorite Illustration of
ROBERT J. LITTLE, Radio Pastor
Moody Bible Institute
Chicago, Illinois

HE WAS IN A HURRY TO BE SAVED

Mark 10:17 says, "And when he was gone forth into the way, there came one running, and kneeled to him, and asked him, Good Master, what shall I do that I may inherit eternal life?" I like that word *running*. I am always glad to see somebody get in a hurry to be saved. I am thrilled when the Spirit of God gets such a grip on a man's heart he cannot wait to get to Jesus.

In a meeting sometime ago in the Faith Baptist Church in Elkhart, Indiana, a high school boy who was a football player came to the services. He was not interested in this evangelist. He was not especially interested in the church. I'll tell you what he was interested in. In that church was a certain blue-eyed, blond young lady and she is what he was interested in. It was her church and her revival and she was attending the services. If he wanted to be near her, he had to be there, too. So there he was.

Like so many young folks do, they sat in the back. Why in the world? Why don't young people come down to the front? Why don't they bring a Bible, a notebook, and pencil and take some notes and get some good out of the service? But young people like to sit in the back of the church. As long as they behave themselves, I do not mind. But I noticed during the song service they were carrying on back there. When it came time for the message, they were still cutting up and laughing and making noise. It was disturbing some folks who needed to hear.

I hate to do it, but I will if I have to. I stopped in the middle of my message and brought my hand down hard on the pulpit. It sounded like a pistol shot. Everyone got quiet right now. It was just as though everyone had just died. Without looking at anyone in particular, I just said, "Now, I have had all I am going to take out of that back row." All over that crowd heads began to turn. Mothers and fathers were looking around to see whose kid it was making the fuss and disturbing the meeting. I went on with the message and had no more disturbance. I gave an invitation and some people got saved. We dismissed the crowd. The next night I was on the platform watching the crowd gather. As I looked out over the crowd I noticed that the same blue-eyed, blond young lady was back again. But somehow between last night and tonight someone had done some tall talking. She was not sitting in the back row now, she was in the second row. If that tall high school football player wanted to be near her, he had to be there, too. So there he was right under the gun. It seemed to him as though every time I drove home a point it was right there, right where he was sitting. He wiggled and squirmed through the entire service. He just could not find a comfortable place on that bench.

At the end of the message I asked for heads to be bowed and eyes to be closed. Then I said, "How many here want to be saved? Lift your hand so that I may see it." It was as though his arm had a spring and I had pulled the trigger. It went up like a flash. I asked for others and others were raised. We prayed. Then I announced that we would sing an invitation song and that the pastor would come and stand in front of the communion table, which was on the floor in front of the pulpit. I said, "You come and take the preacher by the hand and tell him you want to be saved. Let someone come with a Bible and show you from God's Word how you can be saved and know it. Don't hesitate. Come right now on the first word of the first verse."

The pianist hit the note. The crowd stood and began to sing. Now, this boy did not have far to come. But he was a football player. By the time he reached the front he was coming on. He hit the preacher and threw his arms over his shoulders. (He almost knocked him over the communion table.) He buried his head in the preacher's shoulder and broke out sobbing. "Preacher, I've just got to be saved. I can't wait any longer."

And he got it, too. He ran to Jesus and got saved.

The Favorite Illustration of
BUD LYLES, Evangelist
Murfreesboro, Tennessee

ROBED IN THE RIGHTEOUSNESS OF CHRIST

To be saved means that by faith you believe God can clothe you in His own righteousness. Hallelujah, that is what happens! When you get saved, the Lord clothes you in the righteousness of God and when the Lord looks on us through Jesus and His blood and sees us clothed in His righteousness, He sees us clothed as perfect as Jesus Christ Himself. That is our position. That is not our state — none of us is perfect — but that *is* our position, clothed in the righeousness of God.

One of the most wonderful illustrations of this is a story that I heard Dr. Harry Ironside tell. Dr. Ironside was a great Bible preacher. He said that one time down in Texas he was visiting on a sheep ranch. He saw what was the strangest looking thing he thought he had ever seen.

It looked like a little lamb that had four front feet instead of two, four back feet instead of two, and it almost looked like it had two heads — a freakish looking thing. Dr. Ironside stood gazing at it and the sheep rancher said, "Preacher, let me tell you the story of that little lamb because I think it illustrates what you preach and what you believe."

The rancher said, "We had a sheep bear a lamb and the baby lamb died. Then we had another sheep bear a lamb and the mother died. So we thought we would take the lamb that had no mother and put her with the sheep that had lost her lamb and that she would adopt the little lamb whose mother died when it was born. This was just a perfect situation."

The rancher said, "We put that lamb with the sheep that had lost her lamb and she put her head down and she repelled it and repulsed it. She pushed it away and would have no part of the little lamb. It was as if she were saying that it was not hers and no kin to her and she didn't want the lamb."

Then someone suggested, "I know how you can get that mother to adopt that little lamb. You skin that dead lamb and drape it over that little lamb's body and then put it back in the pen and see what happens."

The rancher said, "That is exactly what we did. We clothed that lamb that had no mother in the skin of the lamb who had died. We then placed it in with that mother sheep and that sheep began to love it and she said in substance, 'This is mine.'"

The sheep took in the lamb as if to say, "This lamb is a part of me, this belongs to me, this is mine."

They said, "She is raising that little lamb because it is clothed in the garments of her own."

Thank God, that is what God is doing. God has taken me as his child because I am clothed in the garments of His own. That is the gospel of this Bible. When you are saved, you are robed in the righteousness of Jesus Christ.

The Favorite Illustration of
Tom Malone, Pastor
Emmanuel Baptist Church
Pontiac, Michigan

STOP THAT TRUCK

Three men sat on a bench under an elm tree near the center of town. A tractor-trailer braked for a red light. Gold lettering on the black cab read, "CALL BERKSHIRE'S FOR EFFICIENT SERVICE." The truck's cargo was covered completely with a tarpaulin.

The first man wagged his head and muttered, "We get pensions, we get medicare, we get social security, but we still got that truck."

The second man said, "What's the matter with that truck?"

The third man stared at the truck but said nothing.

The first man said, "That truck pulls into town every Monday and Thursday, regular as clockwork. If some politician would promise to get rid of that truck, I'd vote for him ten times — even a hundred if I could get away with it."

"You're talking foolishness," the second man said. "That truck has a right to come every day it wants to."

The third man looked at the sky but said nothing.

"I heard a politician say the day was coming when a body would be taken care of from the cradle to the grave. I want to hear one of them say he'll do something about the grave and afterwards," said the first man.

"What are you talking about? What's that truck got to do with your grave?"

The third man kicked the dust but said nothing.

The first man clenched his fists and shook it at the disappearing truck. "That there truck is loaded with coffins; empty coffins. There's an awful steady market for them in this town. Those coffins come in here empty and go out full. One of these days I'll be going out of town in one of them. Every time I see that truck I wonder whether it's got mine aboard. I don't want to go out in one of them. I sure wish something could be done."

The second man said, "I've seen that truck every week for years. I never knowed it carried coffins."

The third man brushed away a fly that landed on his knee but said nothing.

The first man said, "Every time I see that truck it makes me blue. If a body could just be sure when he goes it would be a pleasant journey to a pleasant place, it wouldn't be so bad."

The second man shook his head slowly and said, "I don't like to think of some of the things I've done in the past. If there's a hell, it would have been better if I had not been born."

The third man groaned and whispered, "I'm going home," and walked away.

The first man asked, "What's eating him?"

The second man said, "You know he buried his wife this past month."

"That's right, I clean forgot," the first man said. "I'm getting old."

The second man stood up and said, "Come on, we'd better get a beer. It keeps a person from thinking too much."

It's too bad a fourth man with knowledge was not sitting on that bench. He could have said, "It's true, politicians do a heap of talking about doing things for us from the cradle to the grave; but I know Someone who takes care of a body beyond the grave. He has done something about death. 'Jesus said, "I am the resurrection and the life: he that believeth in me, though he were dead, yet shall he live: And whosoever liveth and believeth in me shall never die . . ." ' (John 11:25-26)."

The Favorite Illustration of
CRAIG MASSEY, Pastor
Des Plaines Bible Church
Des Plaines, Illinois

"I'LL BET THOSE OTHER ANIMALS WERE GOATS"

Returning home in 1952 from a worldwide visit to various mission fields, I had the joy of visiting the land of our Lord. Dr. Joseph Stowell, with whom I was traveling, and I were going by car from Beirut, Lebanon, down to see the cities of Tyre and Sidon. En route we stopped at an orange grove and ate some luscious Lebanese oranges. Since there were no signs such as we see in America concerning littering the highways, we threw our orange rinds into the fields. As we did so a flock led by a shepherd came our way. When they were several hundred feet away a few animals left the shepherd and the flock and ran into the field to get the orange rind.

I used this in a message back in the states and a little boy raised his hand. When I said, "Sonny, what do you want?" he said, "I'll bet those other animals were goats." He was right. He had greater perception than many adults.

"My sheep follow me," said Jesus. The real mark of genuine sheep in the spiritual sense is the fact that there is implanted in the heart a deep-seated desire to follow the Shepherd. The goats of false profession run off for the orange rind of worldly appeal, but the true sheep follow the Shepherd.

The Favorite Illustration of
REGINALD L. MATTHEWS,
Field Representative
General Association of Regular Baptist Churches
Des Plaines, Illinois

BRINGING SOULS TO CHRIST—THE GREATEST BLESSING OF ALL

Next to one's own salvation the greatest blessing of all is the salvation of another person. A student, who was at one time enrolled in the Indiana Baptist College, writes this testimony:

> I realized that I was a lost sinner, for Romans 5:12 says, "Wherefore, as by one man sin entered into the world, and death by sin; and so death passed upon all men, for that all have sinned." On April 7, 1960, God gave me a great desire to become a preacher, but at that time I did not know Jesus Christ as my personal Lord and Saviour, therefore, I was not a son of God. Oh, how I thank my brother and personal evangelism teacher. He showed me the way to Jesus, God's only Son, in our class by reading Romans 10:13, which says, "For whosoever shall call upon the name of the Lord shall be saved." I called on the Lord Jesus Christ to be my personal Saviour and now I know I have eternal life.

Christians should never be taken by surprise as to the time and place that lost people receive the Lord. A dear man in a personal evangelism class was under such deep Holy Spirit conviction that he got up from his seat and hurried into another room, broken and crying over his sin. The teacher followed him to the other room and after a few minutes of counsel, brought him back to the classroom. It was there in the classroom that he was shown, again, the plan of salvation, and then both he and his teacher dropped to their knees and he openly called upon the Lord to save him. The other students were all in an attitude of prayer during this time as they experienced this time of great blessing. There could not have been a more practical lesson in soul-winning than the one that was given on that never-to-be-forgotten day. The class was studying the plan of salvation that day as the Lord caused this man to be alarmed about his lost condition.

The next day, the same man brought his well-dressed wife to school. He brought her because he was concerned about her soul. A visiting evangelist asked her if she were a Christian, and she answered in the affirmative. Her answer was really just a way to cover up her lost spiritual condition, to make others think that she was spiritual. Her husband knew better and so did the Lord. A short time later the personal evangelism teacher took both her and her husband into his office. It was in the privacy of this room that the teacher asked her, "Are you really a born-again child of God?" She answered, "Oh, yes." Then the teacher said, "If you are a child of God, you must love the Bible; so let us look at some verses." She was shown various verses regarding the lost condition of man. After reading from two different passages of Scripture, the portion that says, "For all have sinned, and come short of the glory of God" (Rom. 3:23), was read. All of a sudden she sobbed and tears streamed down her cheeks. The question was then asked, "You need to be saved, don't you?" She answered brokenly, "Yes, sir." After being shown God's plan of salvation, she got down on her knees and called upon the Lord to save her.

Dr. G. Campbell Morgan said on one occasion, "The first impulse of a newborn soul is to win another soul to Jesus." This was certainly true of this college student who was saved just the day before. He brought his wife to the place where she too could hear the Lord's plan of salvation and receive the One who saves sinners. Any saved person should be thrilled when another person passes from spiritual death unto life. Any Christian who is right with the Lord has no greater thrill than to have a part in leading souls to Christ. This is the greatest blessing of all and should be the goal of every Christian.

The Favorite Illustration of
LEON F. MAURER, President
Indiana Baptist College
Indianapolis, Indiana

THEIR BEAMING FACES BETRAYED THE SECRET

This story is told regarding the beginnings of the Anaconda Mining Company:

A group of prospectors set out from Bannock, Montana (then capital of the state), in search of gold. They went through many hardships, and several of their little company died en route. Finally they were overtaken by the Indians who took their good horses, leaving them with only a few limping old ponies, and then threatened them, telling them to get back to Bannock and stay there, for if they overtook them again, they would murder the lot of them.

Defeated, discouraged, and downhearted, the prospectors sought to make their way back to the capital city. On one occasion as they tethered out the limping ponies on a creek side, one of the men casually picked up a little stone from the creek bed. He called to his buddy for a hammer, and upon cracking the rock, he said, "It looks as though there may be gold here." The two of them panned gold the rest of the afternoon and managed to realize twelve dollars worth. The entire little company panned gold the next day in the same creek and realized fifty dollars — a great sum in those days. They said to one another: "We have struck it!"

They made their way back to Bannock and vowed not to breathe a word concerning this gold strike — and they energetically kept their word. They quietly set about reequipping themselves with tools and supplies for another prospecting trip. But when they got ready to go back, three hundred men followed them. Who had told on them? No one! The writer of the book — a purely secular columnist — accounted thus for the incident: "Their beaming faces betrayed the secret!"

If we have been enamored with Him whom having not seen we love, we should be unable to conceal the treasure: Our beaming faces should betray the secret.

The Favorite Illustration of
L. E. MAXWELL, President
Prairie Bible Institute
Three Hills, Alberta, Canada

DON'T REJECT GOD'S PARDON

While Andrew Jackson was president of the United States, a man was given a court trial and condemned to die. President Jackson offered to pardon him but the condemned man refused the pardon. Prison authorities, the attorney general of the United States, and others earnestly endeavored to convince the man to accept the pardon. They tried to impress upon him that it would not only spare his life, but that if he did not accept the pardon, it would be an insult to the president. The man persisted in rejecting the pardon.

The attorney general consulted the Supreme Court of the United States, asking whether legal authorities could not *force* the man to receive the pardon. The court ruled that the pardon was merely a printed statement until the man accepted it. If he rejected the pardon, it remained printed matter.

Every soul out of Christ is a sinner and an eternally lost soul (Rev. 20:11-15). The gospel offers God's pardon through the death, shed blood, and resurrection of Jesus Christ as payment for the penalty certain for every lost soul. If an individual accepts the pardon, his sins — past, present, and future — are atoned for, and he is clothed with God's righteousness in Christ (II Cor. 5:21); but if that individual neglects or rejects that pardon, he will suffer forever in the lake of fire (Rev. 20:15).

The Favorite Illustration of
William McCarrell, Director
Christian Work Center
Cicero, Illinois

ALL HAVE COME SHORT

There's no difference in men, they're all sinners. Now, that doesn't mean that there's no difference in sinners. There's a lot of difference in sinners, some are worse than others. God recognizes that. But I found out the other day, flying over to Phoenix (we had to go up thirty-six thousand feet to get over the front that was moving to the east), that when you look down from that elevation you can't judge the height of hills. In fact, when you get up that high you can't distinguish a molehill from an anthill or from a mountain. They all look the same when you get up there. And when God looks down at you, my beloved, though you may think you're head and shoulders above somebody else, you're on the same level — "all have sinned and come short of the glory of God." I have an old illustration about the game of jumping to Catalina Island. It's about twenty-five miles directly across to Catalina from the pier in Santa Monica. We get to the end of the pier and we run and jump off the end to see who can jump to Catalina. Now up to the present, nobody has made it. There have been some mighty good jumps, but nobody yet has made it. It's a delightful game because when you jump, you get wet, and you can say to the other fellow, "I jumped farther than you did." And it is true. Some jump farther. I see some people that I'm sure could outjump me. But I'll tell you this, if you do you'll get wetter than I will. The farther you jump the wetter you get, but you won't make Catalina. All come short of Catalina although some jump farther than others. "All come short of the glory of God" although some are not as great sinners as others. None have measured up to His standards. And for that reason you and I today need His redemption.

> Your best resolutions must totally be waived,
> Your highest ambitions be crossed;
> You never need think that you will ever be saved,
> Until you've learned you are lost.

The Favorite Illustration of
J. VERNON McGEE, Teacher
Thru the Bible Radio
Los Angeles, California

THEY GAVE AND THEN GOD GAVE

Then it happened! An experience that would be most vivid and yet completely unexplainable to me.

Bea and I attended the gospel tabernacle on Forty-first Street in Astoria, Long Island, New York. A missionary came to minister at our church. He was a converted Irishman with great zeal for our Lord. His one ambition was to return to Ireland in order to present God's Word to his fellow Irishmen. There was something about the tone of his voice that spoke of utter sincerity. His zeal and love for our Lord were unmistakable. After his challenging discourse, the pastor announced that a special offering would be received. As I sat in my seat that evening the Lord spoke to me just as truly as I am endeavoring to communicate with you — "I want you to give everything you have in the offering." The experience was so real that I said, "Lord, everything?" "Yes, everything." I emptied every pocket and gave everything I had that night. After the offering had passed and when we stood to our feet to sing the closing hymn, I turned to Bea and I said, "Honey, I have something I want to tell you." She replied by saying, "And I have something I want to tell you also." The benediction was pronounced and various folks came to shake hands and talk, and finally we made our way toward the front of the church.

We stood on the sidewalk saying good night to various parishioners. Finally, the pastor came out, the lights were turned out, the door of the church was locked, the pastor got in his car and drove away. Bea and I were standing outside on the sidewalk in front of the church and Bea said, "What did you want to tell me?" She insisted that I first tell her what I had on my mind. I said, "Honey, I had a most unusual experience tonight. When the offering was being taken the Lord told me to give everything I had in the collection." "Why, that's exactly what He told me to do!" she exclaimed. I thought for a few moments, and I said, "Bea, did you really give everything in that offering?" She said, in the happiest tone of voice, "Yes, I did." I said, "Bea, are you sure the Lord told you to give everything in that offering?" She replied by asking me the same question. Very dogmatically, I said, "Oh, yes, I know He did." She replied with as much dogmatism that she also knew this to be a fact. I asked her if she realized what this meant, for at that time we lived in Corona, Long Island, which meant double carfare, first the Independent Subway and the Q-66 bus going along Northern Boulevard to where we lived, but we had no carfare and to walk that distance would take many hours. Being absolutely certain of the reality of our experience, we began to walk.

As we walked along Forty-first Street toward Broadway in Astoria just one block from the church Bea suddenly darted for several coins which she plainly saw under the clear light of the lamppost near the corner. "Look, look," she exclaimed, as she showed me the money — several quarters, dimes and nickels. Not only did we have enough carfare to get home, but enough for an ice cream soda as well! Oh, how we rejoiced and what a thrilling experience! This was God, for since that day, Bea and I have traveled hundreds of thousands of miles to many states, cities, towns, and villages, and we have never found one single cent under any lamppost anywhere. This was not a coincidence; it was a miracle.

The Favorite Illustration of
RALPH MONTANUS, President-Founder
The Gospel Association for the Blind, Inc.
College Point, New York

"WHEN MEN DIE, CAN WE SLEEP?"

A preacher and his young son were returning home after a meeting in a distant city. As they were traveling along, a car passed them on a hill. There was the squeal of tires, the crash of steel, and the sound of broken glass as an approaching car collided head-on with the car that was passing the pastor and his son.

When they could no longer be of help, the pastor and his young son continued homeward. For the remainder of the trip the boy sat stunned, seemingly reliving the experience over and over — the screams of agony and the dying of the occupants of the cars had made a tremendous impression on him. The father was concerned not only about the eternal destiny of the people who had died but also about his impressionable son who had witnessed such a horrible thing.

Naturally the boy could not eat when they arrived home. He went to bed early. The father became even more concerned about his son for he still had not spoken. In the middle of the night the young boy cried aloud. His father went to his aid.

The father asked, "Son, can't you sleep?"

The boy replied, "Daddy, when men die, can we sleep?"

Even to us as Christians death seems so remote. We pass people everyday who are dying, and yet we seem so unconcerned.

> *The Favorite Illustration of*
> Bob Moore, Pastor
> Marietta Baptist Tabernacle
> Marietta, Georgia

THE SCARLET WORM

The truth that spiritual, eternal life can only be attained on the basis of the suffering and death of the Creator of life is symbolized everywhere in the world of nature by the fact that even the birth of a new physical life must always be preceded by a time of travail and willingness to die on the part of the mother.

One of the most poignant illustrations of this truth is found in Psalm 22:6. This psalm, of course, is the great portrait of the sufferings of Christ on the cross, written a thousand years before they were actually fulfilled. At the height of His sufferings, He cried out: "But I am a worm, and no man; a reproach of men, and despised of the people."

This particular word translated "worm" is the Hebrew *toleah*. It refers to an insect like the cochineal, the females of which produced a substance from which a bright scarlet dye could be extracted. This "scarlet worm," in fact, was the chief source of the scarlet and crimson dyes of antiquity. It was so closely identified with the coloring which was produced from it, that the same word (*toleah,* or its variants, *tola* and *tolaath*) are commonly translated in the Old Testament to read "scarlet" or "crimson."

It may be that the only reason the Lord prophetically identified Himself with this insect was in order to emphasize the extreme humiliation to which He subjected Himself in suffering as our Saviour. More likely, however, He was thinking also of the sacrificial death to which the mother worm submitted herself in order to provide life for the young which she brought forth.

For the mother *toleah,* the "scarlet worm," affixes her body firmly to the trunk of a tree or to a post or similar wooden object so firmly that she can never leave again. After the young are born, her body provides protection for them until they can leave and provide for themselves. And in the process, the mother worm dies, with the scarlet coloring from her dried body imparted to the baby worms and to the tree on which she died.

Although the Lord Jesus was the Son of *man,* it is by Him that men are born to spiritual life. "For it became him, for whom are all things, and by whom are all things, in bringing many sons unto glory, to make the captain of their salvation perfect through sufferings" (Heb. 2:10). He is the antitype, the perfect fulfillment of the type represented by the mother worm, and indeed by every mother in the animal kingdom and in the human family, willing to enter into the suffering of travail, and even death if need be, in order that the child might be born. "He shall see of the travail of His soul, and shall be satisfied" (Isa 53:11).

Looking at the lifeless form of the mother worm impaled on the tree, stained blood-red in token of her suffering and death, we see a host of newborn creatures emerging from the scene of sacrifice, vibrant with life and, hopefully, filled with gratitude to the one who thus laid down her life that they might live. It is peculiarly appropriate that the twenty-second Psalm ends with a prophetic testimony: "A seed shall serve Him; it shall be accounted to [better, "of"] the Lord for a generation. They shall come, and declare His righteousness unto a people that shall be born, that He hath done this."

> *The Favorite Illustration of*
> HENRY MORRIS, Director
> Creation Science Research Center
> San Diego, California

"REACH OUT AND ACCEPT THE MESSAGE WHEN THE TIME IS THERE"

On a seacoast where there are high cliffs two men were gathering birds' eggs to sell. One would remain on the top of the cliff and let the other down on a rope with a little seat attached. One day as the man was being lowered over the cliff he saw a large nest of eggs way back under a sort of overhang. He realized that by swinging himself much as a child does, he could manage to reach the ledge where the nest was perched. After swinging some time he managed to reach the ledge and began gathering the eggs. In his excitement he let the rope slip from his fingers. Now he was on a ledge high above the sea, he could not climb up, and he could not reach the rope. After a while the wind began to blow gently. The rope seat began to move. The wind grew stronger, the seat moved ever closer. The man realized that if the wind would just continue to blow, the seat would continue to swing even more closely, he could by leaping out into space reach the rope. The wind continued to blow, the seat moved closer, and at just the right moment the man leaped, reached the rope and was saved. The rope is the message of salvation, the wind is the Holy Spirit. By many ways He moves the message, the hope of salvation, near us. We must reach out and accept the message when the time is there!

The Favorite Illustration of
ORD L. MORROW,
Associate Radio Minister
Back to the Bible Broadcast
Lincoln, Nebraska

EVANGELICAL ATHEISM

I once counseled with a well-respected evangelical minister. He was fundamental in all his doctrines and preached the Word of God with much authority. He stood up for the Scriptures and was against the many evils of his city. He was somewhat of a fighter and was always looking for an opportunity to play the role of a biblical prophet. One day he came to my office complaining of the difficult time he was having with his associate minister's wife. It seems that she was spreading many rumors through her gossip at the local beauty parlor. After relating his story with much hostility in his voice he said to me, "Narramore, just how far do you carry this forgiveness bit!" I replied, "Seventy-times-seven"; but he didn't seem to get the message. If I had said, "Rev. Jones, just how far do you carry this Virgin Birth bit?" I would have been the subject for the next Sunday morning's sermon. But when it came to a personal frustration near the minister's daily life he was essentially atheistic. Many Christians live this way. We hold to the basic fundamentals of the faith, but in matters of personal living such as hostility, forgiveness, and worry, we really are no different than the atheist.

The Favorite Illustration of
S. BRUCE NARRAMORE, Vice-President
Rosemead Graduate School of Psychology
Rosemead, California

"I GOT OUT FROM BEHIND THE STOVEPIPE"

Life in Christ begins with one's own personal conversion.

I was raised on a ranch in Arizona. Most of the people in our community were ranchers who lived a distance from each other. In this area there was a small church which we attended quite frequently. This little country church was heated by a wood-burning stove which stood near the middle of the room. We didn't need it most of the year, but we never got around to taking it out.

So it was always there with its black stovepipe extending up and out through the roof.

At the age of five or six I began to understand the gospel of Jesus Christ. The minister would talk about heaven. But I didn't like that subject because I had made no preparations to go to such a place. I also disliked his preaching about hell because I had done nothing to sidestep that, either. In fact, I was against nearly everything he talked about. I suppose I wanted to run my own life the way I wished and I didn't want any interference.

Then I began to devise a little plan of my own. I would often sit on the bench behind the stovepipe so the minister could not see me. Somehow I felt that if he wasn't looking me in the face his message would not get through to me. So when he would move to the right I would scoot to the left a little. When he would move to the left I would shift to the right, always keeping the stovepipe between me and the preacher. Now I don't suppose he knew that I even existed, but I was very much aware of *him* and what he was saying! In other words, God's Holy Spirit was seeking an entrance into my life, but I was refusing to yield to Him. The Bible says there are three kinds of stovepipes: (1) the lust of the flesh, (2) the lust of the eyes, and (3) the pride of life. The Word of God teaches that all sin committed or ever considered can be listed as one of these stovepipes. These, of course, are the very things that keep people from trusting Christ as their Saviour. So, for a number of years, whenever

I attended church I tried to sit on the bench behind the stovepipe. Finally, one day, I was riding a horse, driving some cattle into a corral. As I rode along I though about the fact that it was time that I got out from behind the stovepipe and began to transact eternal business with God.

Within a few minutes I got the cattle in the corral, closed the gate, threw the reins over the horse's head, and tied him to a post nearby. Then I knelt down and began transacting eternal business. I said something like this: "God, I believe You made Heaven and earth and people. Therefore I am responsible to You. I know I am a sinner and I believe that Your Son Jesus Christ died for sinners like me. I want You to come into my heart just now and forgive me of my sins. And I will serve You as long as I live. Amen."

I got up from my knees and I was marvelously saved.

The Favorite Illustration of
CLYDE NARRAMORE, Founder-President
Narramore Christian Foundation
Rosemead, California

HE BECAME POOR THAT WE MIGHT BECOME RICH

"For ye know the grace of our Lord Jesus Christ, that, though he was rich, yet for your sakes he became poor, that ye through his poverty might be rich" (II Cor. 8:9).

In my early ministry I printed a church bulletin one Saturday that had as its frontispiece a picture of Christ at the age of twelve (supposedly). I remember it so well. He wore a purple garment decorated with a golden stole. My sister-in-law, who at the time was but a child looked at the picture on the front and exclaimed, "My, He must have been rich!" When I heard that remark, I decided never to use that bulletin again, for it told a lie.

Christ was not rich on earth — although He had been rich in heaven. The verse proves His preexistence. On earth He was poor, voluntarily poor. He was known as a carpenter and He left His trade to be an itinerant preacher and a friend of man and to fulfill His office as the Saviour of the world. He said, "The foxes have holes, and the birds of the air have nests; but the Son of man hath not where to lay his head." He ate and slept in the homes of others or stayed out on the mountainside or by the seaside. When He died, He was buried in another man's tomb. He was poor.

But there was a greater poverty — the poverty of rejection by men, who considered Him demon-possessed and an imposter, one who was harmful to society. The greatest poverty of all was expressed in His words from the cross, "My God, my God, Why hast Thou forsaken me?" He became poor that we through His poverty might become rich, and through Him we have become as rich as He was poor for our sakes.

The Favorite Illustration of
DAVID NETTLETON, President
Faith Baptist Bible College
Ankeny, Iowa

A CONSTANT "BURIAL"

" . . . but if ye through the Spirit do mortify the deeds of the body, ye shall live" (Rom. 8:13b).

This great potential of Christian life is also commanded in Colossians 3:5, and explained as to practice in Romans 6: 11-13. It is an act of faith, of course, requiring repetition daily and even hourly, as circumstances (and the flesh) may demand. This need for continual practice reminds me of a boyhood experience at my home in Florida.

Early in the century there were few automobiles in our county; everyone used horses and mules for transportation and field work. Among our livestock was a saddle horse given my father (William R. Newell) by a Kentucky friend, and this horse, Ben, was a family favorite. However, since he was not young when he came to us, it wasn't long before he became too old for service, and finally we had to face the need to assist him out of this life. This meant, of course, that he had to be shot, which none of us could bring ourselves to do.

A visiting friend offered to do this for us, and Father and my brothers and I retired to his study while our friend proceeded to the barn on his mission of mercy. When we heard the shots, we followed him out to the spot where our old friend now lay awaiting interment. Even this turned out to be something of an undertaking for all of us, and I recall that our eyes were moist as we completed the job. Fond recollections of days gone by filled our thoughts.

But we were mistaken in supposing that this was the last we were to see of old Ben. My brother's hunting dogs were usually on the prowl for something to tide them over between feeding times, and before too many days had passed they had discovered Ben's supposed last resting place and had dug up the remains. This of course necessitated a reburial, and this second one was quite different from the first. Our eyes were moist again, but not for the same reason. And no sooner had we covered him up for the second time than the dogs in turn retaliated by exposing the carcass once more.

For a short time thereafter the process settled down into a daily routine, and I recall that the family cook would awaken my younger brother and myself each morning with the reminder that "you must bury Ben before you go to school today."

Unpleasant as it was, that rotting flesh was not to be compared to the stench of our unburied spiritual "flesh" in the eyes of a holy God. And in like manner, we who know the Lord must unceasingly "bury" our members which are upon the earth — by reckoning ourselves "to be dead indeed unto sin, but alive unto God through Jesus Christ our Lord."

The Favorite Illustration of
PHILLIP R. NEWELL, Director
The Great Commission Prayer League
Chicago, Illinois

LOST IN THE GRASS OF CENTRAL AFRICA

It was about four o'clock one afternoon when I set off alone for a short roundup. After an hour's walk along a stretch of pasture land three gazelles were sighted in a hollow of the plain. Taking note of the wind direction I proceeded to stalk the game for range. Then came a pause before lifting my gun. In that pause the wind changed and the gazelles darted away like greyhounds.

Feeling rather tired and disappointed I lay there for a few minutes with my eyes on the lookout. However, these animals suffer from a fatal curiosity and suddenly one of the antelopes reappeared. There was no pause this time and in an instant the gun was at my shoulder. A sharp report was followed by a dull thud. The antelope reeled, then sank on its haunches. But apparently the bullet had only stunned it, and before I could reach the struggling animal it was up and floundering away. Convinced that it would drop again, I reserved my second barrel and gave chase. For a time it kept to the open plain and there was every hope of running it down, but suddenly it darted into some long grass and disappeared. Still nothing daunted, I continued the chase, following the trail of trampled grass.

While all this was going on, two very important things slipped my mind: one was the time, and the other my direction. It was not long before I was reminded of both, for darkness suddenly overtook me, as it very often does in the bush, and with the darkness the difficulty of discerning my whereabouts. I tried to retrace my steps by feeling my way along the trail of trampled grass, but it was useless. To my dismay a dreadful fact had to be faced: I was lost! No one who has not had the experience can imagine the terror produced by such a situation. Lost! A simple word, but one whose meaning is suddenly illuminated by a sense of helplessness, utter loneliness, a sense of being cut off, thrown back on one's self alone. It gives a new meaning to that pregnant statement of Christ: "I came to seek and to save that which was lost." Picture the bleating sheep separated from the flock, in danger of death by the elements or by the wolves. Lost! That is mankind's spiritual plight. I knew it that night as I wandered through the long grass of Central Africa, miles from anywhere — lost! Nevertheless, it was not until the realization of my utter helplessness came before me that I sought the only reliable source of help — God. Surely it is not without significance that the soul of man, when really isolated and outside the reach of human aid, cries out for God! This fact gives testimony to the other fact that God *is,* and is ready to respond to the cry of the lost soul. Paul knew this when he wrote: "Whosoever shall call [cry out in distress] upon the name of the Lord shall be saved [delivered]" (Rom. 10:13). How apt is the gospel of the Lord Jesus Christ! It just fits the human need at its deepest level!

So I asked God for guidance and help. Nor did He fail to regard my request, for in a remarkably short time after that I reached the open plain again, and with a heart full of gratitude prepared to tackle the remainder of the journey. For a time I tramped on, encouraged by the signal answer to my prayer. But as the darkness deepened and the shrill cries of nocturnal birds seemed to rend the still night air, fear and depression came over me. These feelings deepened when the distant sound of hunting leopards reached my ears. Realizing the possibility of being attacked, I paused to reload my gun. No sooner was this completed than a couple of hunting leopards suddenly appeared a few yards away. The horror of a ghastly death now faced me! It was useless to fire for visibility was too poor for accurate shooting, and a wounded leopard is a formidable enemy. So once again I sought the Lord, and again He listened to my cry, for immediately He made me very conscious of His presence. It seemed to me that my experience just then was similar to Daniel's, who could say with lions all around him, "My God . . . hath shut the lions' mouths."

Suddenly, across the dark plain came a voice — far away but, nevertheless, the voice of someone sent to help me. "Lights! Lights!" I yelled, with a voice that seemed to be strengthened by a supernatural power. "All right," came the answer. Tense moments followed. Then the welcome glare of two powerful motor lamps. How my heart leaped with joy as those beams lit my pathway and scattered my cruel enemies.

In another quarter of an hour or so, completely exhausted, I staggered into camp. My despairing family gathered around me instantly, ministering to my needs, while they rejoiced in the fact that I was safe. Late that night, after recounting my experiences and before turning in for a few hours' sleep, we knelt down to thank the God who is, the God who had delivered me, and who delivers all who call on Him.

Have you ever called on Him? If not, do so now, and experience with thousands of others the joy of being saved (delivered) from your lost condition, and the certainty of being bound for heaven.

The Favorite Illustration of
STEPHEN F. OLFORD, Minister
Calvary Baptist Church
New York, New York

GOD DIRECTED IN WRITING

"God's Simple Plan of Salvation"

I'll never forget the day because it was my twenty-fifth birthday, February 5, 1918. I awoke early that morning and, just as if God spoke aloud to me, I heard, "Ford, I want you to meet with Me in the attic." It was five degrees below zero outside, and I knew the attic wasn't much warmer. But I wrapped myself in heavy clothes, took a pillow to kneel on, and went up to the attic. I spotted the chimney and hurried across the creaking boards to its warm bricks, then huddled down beside it on my knees.

I had not been praying long when I was overcome by the presence of the Holy Spirit. I was moved to tears and cried out, "O God, give me a ministry that will encircle the world and be carried on long after I am gone." I had no idea how the prayer might be answered.

The next morning I got up early again to pray, and this time I asked God to give me an institution for training people to be soulwinners and to prepare for the ministry, missionary service, and other Christian work. The answers to these two prayers didn't come immediately, but they came in a wonderful way!

Some time had elapsed after the attic prayer meeting, when one morning as I was bicycling down the street I approached a boy about eighteen years of age who was waiting for a street car. I thought, "Is that young man saved?" The Lord said to me, "Go and ask him." I wheeled to a stop and asked, "Young man, are you saved?" He said, "No, I am not, but my mother has been talking to me a great deal about being saved." I said, "You would like to be saved, wouldn't you?"

He said, "Yes, I would." "You would like to be saved right now, wouldn't you?" I asked. "Yes, I would," he said.

The street car was stopping at each corner to pick up passengers, and I realized I'd have to hurry to accomplish my goal. I led the young man along the "Romans road" — the verses in Romans about sin, confession, and salvation. He listened carefully and followed each step. Then I asked him, "Will you take my hand and say, 'I will receive the Lord Jesus Christ as my personal Saviour?'" He gripped my hand firmly and said, "I will receive the Lord Jesus Christ as my personal Saviour." I said, "Let's have prayer," and just as we finished the street car arrived and he ran and jumped on. He raised his arm and called, "Mister, I want to thank you for what you did for me." I answered, "If anything was done, God sure did it." And he was gone.

I got on my bicycle and pedaled down the street, saying to myself, "Why, that young man was not saved! You can't lead a soul to Christ in a couple of minutes!" I feared this was true, though I hoped otherwise.

About six months later I was riding a street car on that same street when I noticed a young man in the back seat with a pair of crutches across his knees. I walked back to him, put my hand on his shoulder and said, "Young man, are you saved?" He smiled and said, "Yes, sir, I am saved. You know, I had a very peculiar experience. Sometime ago I was standing down here on the corner waiting for a street car and someone riding a bicycle came along and asked me if I was saved. I do not know who he was, and when he stopped I was not saved, but when he left I sure was, and I am certainly glad for it."

I was overcome. Tears of joy streamed down my face, and I took him by the hand and said, "I'm so glad to hear you say that, for I am the one who was talking to you. It took place in such a short time that I thought you surely couldn't be saved." But again he assured me he belonged to Christ.

That experience convinced me that conversion must be done by the Holy Spirit. No person can save another, but the Holy Spirit can and will when He is given an opportunity to work. This was a thrilling answer to prayer as I had been asking

God each morning to help me reach some soul for Him that day. I knew then that God could accomplish spiritual rebirth in a short time through His Word.

I became a minister of the gospel and pastor of the First Baptist Church in Princeton, Indiana, and continued to witness to individuals to lead them to Christ. One day in 1933 the burden to reach more people became very heavy, and I thought there must be a faster method. There must be a gospel tract that gives the plan of salvation in a simple and clear way. I wrote to the leading tract publishers and asked for all their tracts containing the biblical plan of salvation.

Many answered my request, and I got down on my knees in my office and asked God to show me if I should use one of these tracts. I read each one and asked God, "Is this the one You want me to use?" The answer was, "No." One after another met the same response. So I said, "All right, Father. If You want me to write a tract, You will have to give it to me."

I got up off my knees, picked up a pencil and wrote out a tract almost entirely made up of Scripture verses. Each morning afterward for a week I put the manuscript on a chair, knelt beside it, and asked God if there were any changes He would have me make in the tract. A few changes were made during that week, and a few later, but the tract "God's Simple Plan of Salvation" is practically the same today as it was on the first writing.

With little money to print the tract, I went to J. W. Paul, one of the men at our church and a linotype operator on the newspaper, and asked him to set the type to save that expense. He agreed to this and asked me how many copies I wanted. I said two thousand. He said, "Why, Preacher, don't you want more than that?" I said, "No, I'm sure that will be all we'll need. They tell me there are eighteen hundred homes here in Princeton and I want to put one in each. I do not want to leave here someday without witnessing for Jesus in every home. I'm sure I can get rid of the other two hundred."

God must have laughed at that. Little did I realize that He was beginning to answer my attic prayer in a worldwide way.

The two thousand were printed and wrapped in two packages. I was carrying one in each hand as I came near the church, and then the Lord said, "Ford, do not put these in the homes immediately as you planned, but go into your office and put a tract in each letter you answer."

I did this, and in a few days requests for additional copies came in, some for a few, some for fifty, and one for five hundred. The two thousand copies were soon gone. I went back to the printer and told him to print five thousand. They were soon gone also. Another ten thousand didn't last long either. I covered Princeton with the tracts, but the world seemed to be calling for them. In two years two hundred twenty-five thousand had been given to Christian workers for distribution, and in seven years five million!

One day a letter came from a young man in Milwaukee asking if he could have the tract translated into German. I told him to go ahead. Then a request came from Mexico asking me to allow translation into Spanish. A letter from Brazil requested permission to put the tract into Portuguese. Peter Deyneka of the Slavic Gospel Mission asked if he could translate it into Russian. James Stewart, of the European Evangelistic Crusade, said his committee would make translations into every European language if we would pay for the tracts. Dr. Paul Gupta had the tract translated into many of the languages of India.

Today the tract is being printed in eighty languages, plus Braille for the blind. Every now and then someone asks, "How did you get your tract translated into so many languages?" All we can say is, "God did it." We surely couldn't have done it, and the glory all belongs to Him. Including the copies printed in newspapers and some national magazines such as *Life*, nearly two hundred fifty million copies have been printed in practically every country around the world. This is God's answer to the attic prayer on that frigid morning more than fifty-three years ago.

We have heard from tens of thousands of people who have been saved through reading "God's Simple Plan of Salvation." One lady told us she had led eighty-four people to faith in Christ by using the tract! We have received many similar testimonies, some with astonishing stories. Kurt Wagner, Hitler's bodyguard, was saved through reading the tract in the German language. He is now in the full time gospel ministry.

Al Johnson, Topeka, Kansas, a bank robber, was saved after reading the tract which came to him anonymously in the mail. Our film *The Way Out* dramatically depicts this amazing true story. A Japanese couple was saved from suicide at Mount Aso through reading this tract in the Japanese language. Our film *Suicide Mountain* portrays this heart-touching true story. We give God all the praise and glory. We keep no record. We will wait to see all that God has done when we meet Him above. What a day of rejoicing that will be!

The Favorite Illustration of
FORD PORTER, Interim Pastor
Lifegate Baptist Church
Indianapolis, Indiana

ONLY TWO DOORS AWAY FROM BLESSING

My wife and I were scheduled to fly from Miami by Eastern Airlines to St. Thomas in the Virgin Islands where I was to speak at a baccalaureate and commencement service in the Blue Water Bible College. We were told in Miami that due to storms in the islands the airport there was flooded and it was not possible for us to land. It would be necessary, they said, to take a different flight to San Juan, Puerto Rico, from which we would fly by seaplane to St. Thomas. On arrival in San Juan, we were told that the water on St. Thomas had cleared and that we could land there after all!

We took off in a small plane but soon flew into gathering clouds. The pilot and copilot looked at one another questioningly, spoke in Spanish, acted bewildered, and turned back to San Juan. Later that evening we took off again in a larger plane and finally landed on St. Thomas at the exact time I was supposed to speak at a graduation banquet! I had no idea where the banquet was being held. For two hours we tried unsuccessfully to reach the pastor by phone. We were in a strange land with no car, no contacts, and the one person we knew could not be reached! We were tired, miserable, and very hungry as we thought about the banquet we could not find.

Late that evening we found a cab driver who could speak English and he took us to the home of the pastor, who with his family had just returned from the banquet. To our chagrin, we learned that the banquet had been in an island hotel just *two doors away* from the airport — within easy walking distance of where we had been sitting all evening!

How many of God's choice blessings are near at hand and we are not aware of them because of our ignorance or unbelief. How many will remain lost throughout all eternity even though they were really only "two doors away" from the bounty and blessing of the gospel feast!

> *The Favorite Illustration of*
> HUGH PYLE, Pastor
> Central Baptist Church
> Panama City, Florida

OVER THREE HUNDRED MILES TO FIND SOMEONE TO WIN HER SONS!

On the last Thursday in June a few years ago, a family of five — father, mother, and three sons — drove from Southern Ohio to Wheaton, Illinois, to see me. The good woman had written to find when I would be at home. "My three sons are not saved and I do not know where to go to have someone tell them how to be saved. I have read your book on *Prayer,* and I have read copies of *The Sword of the Lord,* and I know you are a man of God whom I can trust. When could you see us and talk to my three boys?"

I had my secretary write that I would be at home three certain days soon, and would be glad to see the family at any time they could come, day or night, in those three days.

So on that Thursday about seven in the evening I met them at my home in Wheaton. She explained again how deeply concerned she was for her sons to be saved. I suppose the youngest was about twelve; the other two in their teens.

I began carefully talking to the young lad. I found that in a Church of God Sunday school he had made a profession of faith. As we went carefully into the Scriptures, showing that all have sinned and so one needs to be born again and have a new heart, and that Christ had died for him and if he would trust Jesus Christ and depend on Him, he would have his sins forgiven and become a child of God, he brightened up and came to see that that was what he had done, although, before, he had had no assurance of salvation. I went into such careful detail that the good mother, a little troubled, thinking they might be imposing on me, said, "Brother Rice, we are late and you are tired. Would you rather we would go to the motel now and see you again in the morning?"

"Oh no," I said, "let us get this matter settled tonight."

"But I have some other things I want to talk to you about anyway," she said.

I continued with the other boys. First, I went into the truth that all have sinned and come short of the glory of God and so that each one is a lost sinner by nature, needing to be converted, to be born again. I showed from John 3:16 that God loves the sinner, that Christ died for our sins and that now one should trust Jesus to forgive him and save him. When he honestly admitted he was a lost sinner and wanted to be saved, I suggested that we pray and put his desire into words. I told about the publican in Luke 18 who went up to the temple to pray and said, "God be merciful to me a sinner," and how he went home saved, justified that day.

He prayed the same prayer humbly. "God be merciful to me a sinner."

Now I suggested that he add to that, "And save me for Jesus' sake." And he did.

Then I said, "You have admitted you are a sinner and have asked God for mercy and forgiveness. Now He says that if you will believe on Him and rely on Him, He will give you everlasting life. Are you ready to do that now?" Yes, he was.

Then I suggested, "If you will here and now take Christ as your own personal Saviour, depending on Him to forgive you and save you as He promised, I suggest that you take my hand as a sign between you and your mother and your

107

dad and your brothers and God and me, that you are now accepting Christ's offer of forgiveness and are trusting Him as your own personal Saviour and that you will set out to claim Him and live for Him. Will you do it?"

Yes, he would, and gladly we shook hands on the matter. Then I showed him John 3:36, "He that believeth on the Son hath everlasting life. . . ."

I said, "Have you trusted Christ to save you? Have you believed on Him, relied on Him in this matter?"

"Yes," he said.

And I said, "What do you have?"

Looking at that blessed Scripture (the Scripture that years ago had led me into light and assurance after three sad years of doubt), he said, "Why, that says I have everlasting life!" And so he claimed the Lord openly before his family.

Then I began with the other boy, step-by-step, and the third son trusted Christ and claimed Him openly and happily.

I turned then to the mother and said, "You said there was something else you wanted to talk to me about, too?"

She pointed her thumb to her husband and then to herself and said, "We are not saved either!"

So I began at the same Scriptures again and taught them how to trust Christ, and they too asked God to be merciful to them and they too trusted Him to forgive them.

They were a happy family! All were assured that they were God's children and now together were going to heaven.

The next morning they came by the office to see me and we had prayer before they returned to their home fifty miles from Dayton.

Before they left, that good wife and mother said, "Now, Brother Rice, let me see if I have this right. It seems to me from what you told me and from what the Bible says as you explained it, that when a person is sick and tired of sin and really wants forgiveness and when he believes that Jesus died for him and is ready to save him, and when he trusts Him to do it, right then he has got it. Is that right?"

"Yes," I said, "that is right and you have got it!"

Then she said a strange thing — "It seems like people ought to be able to tell it!" She wanted to be able to tell others

out to live for Jesus Christ. The last time I heard, they belonged to a church in Houston, Texas, and were serving God.

The Favorite Illustration of
LEE ROBERSON, Pastor
Highland Park Baptist Church
Chattanooga, Tennessee

"GROUNDED" BY THE PLEASURES OF THIS WORLD

Titus 2:12 reads "Teaching us that, denying ungodliness and worldly lusts, we should live soberly, righteously, and godly in this present world." This is the life that pleases our Lord. But our adversary, the devil, carries on an endless warfare to defeat the very purposes of God for our lives.

What happens when a Christian yields to the suggestions of the evil one? In II Timothy 4:10, with sorrow the apostle writes, ". . . Demas hath forsaken me, having loved this present world. . . . " Earlier, in Colossians 4:14 and Philemon 24, Paul commends Demas as a fellow-laborer. No doubt Demas was a born-again Christian. But the pleasures of this world "grounded" him and power for godly living and fellowship was short-circuited.

Some time ago, at the height of a Saturday night meeting at Pacific Garden Mission, all the lights went out. I immediately sensed that a main fuse had blown. After clearing the trouble I picked up a 100-ampere fuse and hurried to the main switch box. I soon found the blown fuse, replaced it with the new one, and all was light again. I looked at the blown fuse in my hand and remarked, "How like a worldly Christian is a blown fuse." Though it is still connected to the source of energy, power cannot get through because the circuit is broken. Thus it is with the Christian who loves this present world. All his "fuses" are blown and his light has gone out. On God's side he is still connected to heaven but light and power for victorious living cannot get through because he is *grounded*.

But there is recovery in the grace of God — I John 1:9. Fellowship is renewed and all power in heaven and in earth is

111

available to live soberly, righteously, and godly in this present evil world.

The Favorite Illustration of
HARRY G. SAULNIER, Superintendent
Pacific Garden Mission
Chicago, Illinois

THE DIFFERENCE BETWEEN COVERING SIN AND TAKING IT AWAY

My favorite illustration is one I heard Dr. Monroe Parker tell in a sermon contrasting the "covering" of sin in the Old Testament and the "taking away" of sin in the New Testament.

He said that he once heard the late Harry Rimmer say substantially this:

I was in a city on a summer Sunday, where I was to speak at a Bible conference three times that day. I arose in the morning and dressed in a white linen suit — the only suit I had with me. I then went down to the hotel dining room for breakfast. I had a glass of loganberry juice. I got a spot of it on the lapel of that linen suit.

When I finished breakfast I went to my room and put some talcum powder on the spot. It worked. But by time for the afternoon service, the spot had reappeared. I put more talcum powder on it. It worked. But by time for the night service the spot had reappeared. I put more talcum powder on it. It worked.

I *atoned* (covered) for that spot three times. But on Monday morning I sent that suit to the cleaners and had that spot *expiated*.

The Favorite Illusration of
NOEL SMITH, Editor
Baptist Bible Tribune
Springfield, Missouri

GOD'S WAY UP IS DOWN"

Will you pardon me if I tell you in as humble a way as I can how God broke me? It was in the very early years of my ministry. After graduating from seminary, I went directly to a large Presbyterian church in Toronto, where I was pastor for some three and a half years. The church held eighteen hundred people and I saw it packed to capacity again and again.

One day I resigned. It never dawned on me for one single moment that there would be any difficulty in securing another church as large as the one I had had. To my amazement I couldn't find a church, I couldn't get a call. I started preaching in smaller churches. But even the small churches didn't want me. My money was disappearing; I had a wife and a child to support. We were not getting sufficient food, we were not able to meet our obligations. I saw starvation facing me. I didn't realize that God was going to break me once and for all. I kept going down and down and down.

That year Paul Rader came to Toronto to hold his first evangelistic campaign. It was held in Massey Hall, then the largest auditorium in the city. With a little glimmer of hope in my heart, I went to the head usher and said, "Will you let me usher during the meetings of this campaign?" The head usher agreed to let me usher and assigned me to the side aisle. Presently I saw the head usher and the assistant usher conferring together and looking in my direction. Then the assistant usher walked right over to my aisle, and without saying anything to me he took over. I sat down in the back seat with tears pouring down my cheeks. I said, "Lord, my ministry is over. All the preparation I have made has been in vain. Nobody wants me. I can't even usher."

After three nights I went to the head personal worker and said, "Will you let me do personal work in this campaign?" "Certainly," he said. I waited for three nights and never once did he nod to me, never once did he give me an opportunity to lead a soul to Christ. After the third night I walked to the back of the auditorium and sat down. Again tears poured from my eyes, my heart was broken. I said, "Lord, it's all over. I'll never again be able to preach. It's quite evident I've been laid on the shelf."

Three days later I said, "I'll make one last attempt. If this fails, then I'm finished and I'll take it as an indication that God doesn't want me in the ministry." So I went to the man who was in charge of the bookstand. The ushers went up and down the aisles selling hymnbooks, so I said, "Will you allow me to sell hymnbooks in the aisles?" He said, "Yes." He loaded me with an armful of books, hymnbooks that had been published by Arthur W. McKee. Suddenly something happened. Arthur W. McKee, who was leading the singing, stepped to the front of the platform and said, "Tonight we're going to sing a new hymn, one that has been published in this hymnbook for the first time. It's entitled 'Saved! Saved! Saved!'" Then he did something I'll never forget. He pointed to where I was selling hymnbooks and said, "Do you see that young man down there selling hymnbooks?" Everybody looked in my direction. "That young man wrote this hymn." I wanted the floor to open and let me through. I stopped selling hymnbooks as quickly as I could and got out of sight.

I'll never forget the singing of that hymn. It seemed as though the roof of Massey Hall was going to be lifted as that great choir of some five hundred voices and that audience sang that song for the first time. "And now I'm saved eternally, I'm saved, saved, saved." It was my personal testimony. I went back to my home with a new joy in my heart. I said, "Lord, I'm not on the shelf, You haven't given me up. You've simply been breaking me. I've been so proud, You couldn't trust me."

Suddenly, to my utter amazement, I received a cable from the great Spurgeon's Tabernacle in London, asking me if I would cross the Atlantic Ocean and occupy their pulpit for some weeks. Without a moment's hesitation I agreed to go. After fulfilling that mission I came back to Toronto, and then the calls started coming in. The work in Toronto opened up, and from that day to this I've had to turn down about twenty invitations for every one that I've been able to accept. God did the exceedingly abundant. He knew the plan for the future. He knew that the People's Church would be founded in

Toronto. He knew there would be a worldwide missionary work. But He had to prepare the instrument, He had to humble me, He had to break me. I had to go down, for God's way up is down.

The Favorite Illustration of
OSWALD J. SMITH, Minister of Missions
The Peoples Church
Willowdale, Ontario, Canada

MASTER BALONEY

When the city police found a tender three-year-old lad walking down the streets of Phoenix, Arizona, they figured he was big enough to at least partially identify himself.

The desk sergeant kindly queried, "What's your name, Sonny?"

"*Baloney!*" declared the youngster.

"Please," the sergeant pleaded, "tell me your real name."

"*Baloney,*" was the reply. They tried bribes, but nothing worked. The mystery lad ate a candy bar and refused to change his story.

In the process of time a lady called, voice quivering and filled with anxiety, to ask the police to help her find her lost son. Assuring her that he had already been found, the inquisitive officer asked, "What's his name, Ma'am?"

"*Baloney,*" replied the woman.

That boy has started learning the hard lesson early in life — that folks will not believe you sometimes, even when you are right. No one believed Columbus, at first, *but he was right!* No one believed Robert Fulton — and how they slapped their thighs with devilish glee at his "foolish" enthusiasm — *but his steamboat worked!* The same was true with the Wright Brothers, Marconi, Edison, and just about everyone else who has ever introduced a theory or fact contrary to public sentiment and belief.

Nowhere is this evidence manifested more clearly than in the proclamation of the truth of salvation by grace through faith. Public sentiment has long held that salvation is a matter of character and goodness. I have dealt personally with literally hundreds of people and have preached to unnumbered thousands of others — as has every other Bible preacher — who felt that being good would gain them glory. The repeated showing of scores of Scriptures did not shake them in their conviction, and truth was disbelieved because it contradicted preconceived ideas.

When it comes to salvation, you had better listen to God! He has declared: "For by grace are ye saved through faith; and that not of yourselves; it is the gift of God: Not of works, lest any man should boast" (Eph. 2:8-9).

The Favorite Illustration of
ROBERT L. SUMNER, Evangelist-Author
Brownsburg, Indiana

Sumner's Incidents and Illustrations, p. 279, Copyright ©, Biblical Evangelism Press, Brownsburg, Indiana; Used by permission.

FORTY WRESTLERS FOR CHRIST

In the days when the ruling passion of the Roman Emperor Nero was to exterminate the Christians, there lived and served him a band of soldiers known as the "Emperor's Wrestlers." Fine, stalwart men they were, picked from the best and the bravest of the land, recruited from the great athletes of the Roman amphitheater.

In the great amphitheater they upheld the arms of the emperor against all challengers. Before each contest they stood before the emperor's throne. Then through the courts of Rome rang the cry: "We, the wrestlers, wrestling for thee, O Emperor, to win for thee the victory and from thee, the victor's crown."

When the great Roman army was sent to fight in faraway Gaul, no soldiers were braver or more loyal than this band of wrestlers led by their centurion Vespasian. But news reached Nero that many Roman soldiers had accepted the Christian faith. To be a Christian meant death, even to those who served Nero best; therefore, this decree was straightway dispatched to the centurion Vespasian: "If there be any among your soldiers who cling to the faith of the Christian, they must die!"

The decree was received in the dead of winter. The soldiers were camped on the shore of a frozen inland lake. The winter had been cruel, but the many hardships they had endured together had served to unite them more closely. It was with sinking heart that Vespasian, the centurion, read the emperor's message. Yet to a soldier there is one word supreme — Duty!

Vespasian called the soldiers together and asked the question: "Are there any among you who cling to the faith of the Christian? If so, let him step forward!" Forty wrestlers instantly stepped forward two paces, respectfully saluted, and stood at attention. Vespasian paused. He had not expected so many, nor such select ones. "The decree has come from your emperor," he said, "that any who cling to the faith of the Christian must die! For the sake of your country, your comrades, and your loved ones, renounce this Christian faith!" Not one of the forty moved. "Until sundown I shall await your answer," said Vespasian. Sundown came. Again the question was asked: "Are there any among you who cling to the faith of the Christian? If so, let him step forward!" Again the forty wrestlers stepped forward and stood at attention.

Vespasian pleaded with them long and earnestly without prevailing upon a single man to deny his Lord. Finally he said, "The decree of the emperor must be obeyed, but I am not willing that your comrades should shed your blood. I am going to order that you march out upon the lake of ice, and I shall leave you there to the mercy of the elements. The warmth of the fire, however, will be waiting to welcome any willing to renounce Christ." The forty wrestlers were stripped and then without a word they wheeled and, falling into columns of four, marched toward the center of the lake of ice. As they marched they broke into the chant of the arena: "Forty wrestlers, wrestling for Thee, O Christ, to win for Thee the victory and from Thee, the victor's crown!" Through the long hours of the night Vespasian stood by his campfire and watched. As he waited through the long night, there came to him fainter and fainter the wrestlers' song.

As morning drew near one figure, overcome by exposure, crept quietly toward the fire; in the extremity of his suffering he had renounced his Lord. Faintly but clearly from the darkness came the song: "Thirty-nine wrestlers, wrestling for

Thee, O Christ, to win for Thee the victory and from Thee, the victor's crown!" Vespasian looked at the figure drawing close to the fire and then out into the darkness whence came the song of faith. Perhaps he saw eternal light shining there toward the center of the lake. Who can say? But off came his helmet and clothing, and he sprang upon the ice, crying, *"Forty* wrestlers, wrestling for Thee, O Christ, to win for Thee the victory and from Thee, the victor's crown!" "For to me to live is Christ, and to die is gain" (Phil. 1:21).

The Favorite Illustration of
PAUL TASSEL,
National Youth Representative
General Association of Regular Baptist
Churches

ARE YOU WAITING AND WATCHING?

"My soul waiteth for the Lord more than they that watch for the morning" (Ps. 130:6).

The expectation of the Christian is for the return of his Lord. It was John Kerr who said, "His coming looks in upon the whole life of His Church, as a lofty mountain peak dominates every little valley and solitary home about its base, and belongs to them all alike. Every generation lies under the pleasant shadow of it."

The psalmist, in awe of God's forgiving mercy, portrays himself as waiting for the Lord to manifest His presence, even as the night watchman yearns for the breaking of dawn. By application, this waiting on the part of the writer symbolizes our expectation of Christ's return. We should anticipate His appearing with the same eagerness.

A lad rushed into his home one Sunday morning. "Mother, what do you think? Jesus is coming again!" "How do you know?" she asked. "My Sunday school teacher told me this morning." "When is He coming?" "Oh, I don't know," responded the boy, "but He *is* coming!" The next day after school, with the words still fresh on his heart, he ran in exclaiming, "Is He here? Is He here, Mother?" "Who?" "Why, Jesus!" said the boy. "Did He come?" "Not yet!" she replied. Disappointment clouded the youngster's face as he said, "I guess I'll go out and play."

It seems to me this has happened to many of God's children. For a while they have looked for Christ's return; but the things of the world have crowded in and discouragement has come, and they're gone out to play. May God rekindle in us this holy attitude of waiting and watching for Christ.

O can we say we are ready, brother?
Ready for the soul's bright Home?
Say, will He find you and me still watching,
Waiting, waiting when the Lord shall come?
— Fanny Crosby

The Favorite Illustration of
PAUL R. VAN GORDER, Associate Teacher
Radio Bible Class
Grand Rapids, Michigan

THE THRILL OF ENTERING HEAVEN

My parents came from the land of Belgium and remained in America. As a result I was reared in a land where I had no relatives because all of them stayed in Europe. When I was twenty-one years of age, my parents went back to Belgium as missionaries and I stayed in the United States to complete my college education. Upon graduation I decided to go to Belgium and see all of my loved ones for the first time. One can imagine the excitement that coursed through my body as I realized that I would see my grandparents, uncles, aunts, and cousins for the first time. My parents wrote that they would all be in Amsterdam, Holland, to await the ocean liner and stated: "We will be in a group waving the American and Belgian flags." I slept little that night because of extreme excitement; morning finally arrived. The announcement was made that within one half-hour land would be sighted — then it was fifteen minutes, then ten, and then five. Finally I saw the group waving the two flags and chills I had never experienced coursed through my body. The loved ones hugged me and showered affection upon me like I had never known. What a climactic mountain-top experience this was in my life! Many times since my thoughts have centered on eternity, as some of those very loved ones are now in the presence of the Lord. One of these days I am going to experience the same thrill as I enter glory to be united with loved ones for all eternity. If all of us could visualize heaven in this manner, it would make Philippians 1:21 very real.

The Favorite Illustration of
JACK VAN IMPE, Evangelist
Royal Oak, Michigan

JESUS FIRST OF ALL

When we think of the glories which we shall enjoy with Him as the eternal ages roll, I am reminded of old John Jasper, that former slave who after the War between the States pastored the Sixth Mt. Zion Baptist Church in Richmond, Virginia. Somebody asked him if there had been five preceding Mt. Zion Baptist Churches and that was why they called it the "Sixth." He said, "No, we just liked the name."

Old John Jasper pastored a great church. He was speaking to his congregation one day on heaven and the joys which will await us on the other side. He tried to describe those beauties, the joys ineffable and full of glory which will be our portion. His vivid imagination and his emotions were caught up and as he opened his mouth to speak he couldn't say a word. He tried several times and the great crowd sat there in anticipatory silence. He tried again and they could see his big Adam's apple working up and down, but still no sound. Then they saw the tears as they began to seep out of the corners of his eyes and roll down his black cheeks. Still as he would try to articulate, not a sound could he make. Finally, he shook his head and waved his crowd toward the exit, but that great audience of black folk just sat there as if enthralled. After several attempts to no avail, he walked back to the side of the pulpit and had his hand upon the door which led to his study, and again he waved the crowd toward the exit but they still sat there.

Seeing that they wouldn't leave, he composed himself and walked back toward the edge of the pulpit and leaning over it said something like this, "Brothers and sisters, when I think of the glory which shall be revealed in us, when I think of the marvelous provisions of God's amazing grace, when I think of the things which eye hath not seen, neither hath ear heard nor entered into the heart of man to even imagine the things that God hath prepared for His own, I can visualize that day when old John Jasper's last battle has been fought and the last burden has been borne. I can visualize that day when this tired servant of God shall lay down his burdens and walk up to the battlements of the City of God. Then as I stand outside the beautiful gate, I can almost hear the Mighty Angel on guard say, 'John Jasper, you want your shoes?'

"I'se gonna say, 'Course I wants ma shoes, ma golden slippers to walk the gold-paved streets of the City of God, but not now.'

"Then I can hear the Mighty Angel as he says, 'John Jasper, don't you want your robe?'

"I'se gonna say, 'Course I wants ma robe, that robe of linen clean and white which am the righteousness of the saints, but not now.'

"Then the Angel would say, 'John Jasper, you want your crown?'

"I shall say, 'Course, Mighty Angel, I wants all the reward that's comin' to me, this poor black servant of the Lamb, but not now.'

"I can hear him as he says, 'John Jasper, would you like to see Moses, the great Law-giver who led God's people out of bondage on the way to the Promised Land?'

"I'se gonna say, 'Course, Mighty Angel, I wants to hear Moses sing the song of Moses and de Lamb, but not now.'

"Then the Angel would say, 'John Jasper, wouldn't you like to see Elijah, the great prophet, who called down fire from heaven, wouldn't you like to shake hands with John the beloved disciple who leaned on the Master's breast at the Last Supper? Wouldn't you like to shake hands with Paul, the great apostle to the Gentiles, the greatest church establisher and soul-winner of all time?'

"I'll say, 'Course, Mighty Angel, I wants to know and to shake hands and to commune with those, the saints of God who have won the incorruptible crown. Yes, I have some loved ones over here I wants to see, too, but not now. Fust, I wants to see Massa Jesus, I wants to see Him fust of all.' "

The Favorite Illustration of
G. BEAUCHAMP VICK, Pastor
Temple Baptist Church
Detroit, Michigan

"HOT DOG, HOT DOG, HOT DOG"

My favorite illustration comes from my own pastoral experience. It took place on Sunday morning at Bible Baptist Church in Elkton, Maryland. The Sunday morning service was just ready to begin when in came a man who had never attended our church before. He looked around with awe and amazement at the great number of people packed into the large auditorium. He had heard about these people and now he had come to see for himself.

He came slowly down the aisle looking from side to side and seated himself on the second row from the front. As I preached he listened with the keenest of interest. When I gave a negative tone to my statements he would shake his head from side to side showing agreement. I asked the question, "Don't you think everybody ought to be saved?" He nodded his head up and down in definite approval. It was not hard to tell how he stood on any issue.

When the invitation time came, I said, "Every eye closed and every head bowed. Now how many of you are not saved, but you would like to be, and you want us to pray for you? Will you raise your hand?" He shot up his hand and waved it back and forth persistently until he was sure that I had seen it. When I asked those who would claim Christ to come forward, he literally bounced out and darted to the altar. One of our men prayed with him and gave him assurance of salvation.

In a moment I asked him to stand. He stood stiff and erect;

he was really into the matter with body, soul and spirit. I asked, "Sir, do you believe that Christ died to save sinners?" "Yes, Sir, I want to do just that," he said rejoicing, with a beam of triumph about him.

When he came into the baptistry, I dropped him into the water and out again to walk in the newness of life. He came up out of the water clapping his hands and shouting, "Hot dog, hot dog, hot dog."

Our people roared with laughter. I quickly asked them for silence as I explained that this poor man had not been around the church and didn't know about "Amen, Praise the Lord, and Hallelujah"; his word was "Hot dog," and he was praising the Lord with the only vocabulary he knew.

> *The Favorite Illustration of*
> TOM WALLACE, Pastor
> Beth Haven Baptist Church
> Louisville, Kentucky

A QUESTION OF KNOWING THE SON OF MAN

While conducting an eight-day Bible conference in a southern city, I was informed by my hotel that due to demand for space I could use their accommodations for only three days of my stay, and that other hotels in the community were equally crowded. A Christian businessman hearing of our problem phoned instructions that after my three days in the hotel I should go to another hotel where space would be available for me.

Arriving at the registration desk, I found a dozen others ahead of me. As each made his request for a room, he was informed they had no space available. Nobody in the line received a room, even though some of them had confirmed reservations. When the clerk took my name, he fumbled through some papers and then replied, "Yes, we have a room for you."

As I contemplated my experience, I asked the question, "Why was I admitted to a lovely hotel room when others had been turned away?" The answer was simple enough. The businessman who had secured the room for me was in a position to do favors for the hotel and they could not afford to turn away a request for one of his friends. I had secured a room on another man's name and another man's favor.

In like manner, Jesus Christ is our way to heaven. As Christ stated it in John 14:6, "No man cometh unto the Father but by me." It is through His name, through His merit, through His acceptability to God the Father that believers in Christ can be assured of going to heaven. In gaining a hotel room, it was a question of knowing the right man. In going to heaven, it is a question of knowing the Son of man.

The Favorite Illustration of
JOHN F. WALVOORD, President
Dallas Theological Seminary
Dallas, Texas

YOU CANNOT CHANGE YOURSELF INTO A CHRISTIAN

Many people today are trying to change themselves into Christians. They remind me of a crow who wanted to be a pigeon. Watching the benefits afforded a number of pigeons at a nearby barnyard, he too longed for the grain and corn they enjoyed. He was smart enough to know he had to change from his old self and decided to work at it. First he splashed in the creek and soaked his feathers. Then he flew sluggishly to a limestone quarry. He perched on a pile of grey limestone dust, and with a mighty flapping of wings he stirred up a crow-sized hurricane. The dust settled all over his feathers, and after drying in the sun, he was a beautiful grey — like a pigeon. All this activity made him tired so he sat and complained . . . and a crow never complains without caws (cause). Excuse the pun, and now back to the changing crow.

Next he tried to change his walk. It took days for him to master the neck-bobbing stride of a pigeon, but finally he did so; and then he turned to the last step of his self-improvement plan, to turn his "caw's" into "coo's." This also took a lot of practice, but at last he achieved a fair-sounding "coo" he felt would be acceptable.

Now he was ready. After carefully checking each self-effected change, he flew over and landed among the pigeons.

He was quickly accepted, and two lady pigeons even began to fight for his attention. The happy days passed and he fooled them all until . . . one afternoon a huge thunderstorm broke over the valley. All the birds fled to a wire under the barn roof, but he was just under the eaves. The wind ruffled his feathers and the rain soaked him until he caught cold. After the storm passed, he was no longer able to deceive the others. His grey color washed off and his voice was again harsh, and the pigeons ran him off.

Many people are trying the same stunt. They dress in manmade respectability and join some church. They strut and sing and chant and creed. They talk the language and by physical and mental labor try to pattern their lives as a Christian. All such need to remember that "man looketh on the outward appearance, but the Lord looketh on the heart" (I Sam. 16:7). All forms of godliness which is just put on will some day come off, for "it is appointed unto men once to die, but after this the judgment" (Heb. 9:27). You cannot change yourself into a Christian. You must by God's power be born into His family. Jesus said, "Ye must be born again" (John 3:7).

> *The Favorite Illustration of*
> HAL WEBB, Evangelist
> Ridley Park, Pennsylvania

THE FOOTPRINTS OF GOD

Psalm 77:19

I was scheduled to speak at the Chicago Moody Founder's Week Conference in early February of 1960. During the latter part of the preceding December I received a letter from Dr. William Culbertson, President of Moody Bible Institute, in which he made a statement to this effect, "Brethren, we must come to Founder's Week with broken hearts if the world is to receive blessing through us." That was an unusual letter from the director of a conference. It gripped me. I paused then and there at my desk and prayed, "O God, I cannot answer for the other speakers who come to Founder's Week.

But I am responsible for the state of my own heart. Lord, I ask you now, whatever the cost may be, to send me to Moody's Founder's Week with a broken heart."

Then just a few days later, at a New Year's watchnight service in Manitoba, Canada, I chose as my year's verse for 1960 Colossians 1:18: "That in all things he might have the preeminence." I spoke that night on the subject "Divine Totalitarianism" emphasizing the fact that Jesus Christ deserves to have a totalitarian place in our lives, that our lives are not to be run by "a two-party government," but under "a state of divine totalitarianism." That night I prayed, "God, make this true in my life during the coming year regardless of what it may cost." Little did I realize what these two brief prayers would cost me and how God was going to answer them.

During January I was scheduled to minister in conferences in the West Indies. On January 27, during the precise time we were gaily celebrating Mr. Epp's birthday at the Myrtle Bank Hotel in Kingston, Jamaica, with some wonderful Christian friends, the Lord reached down into my home in Lincoln, Nebraska, and in a twinkling of an eye took my wife to heaven. About five that afternoon I was contacted by overseas telephone and given the message, "Your wife died of a heart attack at 1:00 P.M." She was to have met me the following Monday in Chicago where we had planned to be at Founder's Week together.

I caught the first plane home, arriving some sixteen hours later. Upon my arrival my assistant at the Back to the Bible office informed me that he had telephoned to Dr. Culbertson at Moody Bible Institute informing him of my wife's sudden death and telling him that I likely would not come to Founder's Week as planned. He now asked should he confirm this cancellation? My immediate reply was in the affirmative. But during the hours of that night God dealt with my soul. He spoke to me saying, "Do you remember Dr. Culbertson's letter? And do you remember how you prayed that day in your office?" He further said, "Do you remember Colossians 1:18, and what you said in Manitoba on New Year's Eve? And how you prayed that night?" It was a difficult struggle for me, but falling to my knees beside my bed I said, "Lord, I will go. You give me the grace and I will speak at Founder's

Week as planned. You have answered my own prayers in a way I never anticipated or thought, but I will accept your answer. I will now do my part, by your grace."

To stand before that huge audience at Founder's Week two days after we had buried my sweet Christian wife was the first step in the victory over what otherwise might have been a crushing defeat.

We never know exactly how God may answer our prayers, and we need to pray with care and with sobriety. But we *must* be obedient to God's will and God's call when it comes to us. And we need always to remember that He never makes mistakes.

O God, glorify Thyself at my expense, and send me the bill . . . anything, Lord, I set no price.

— A. W. Tozer

The Favorite Illustration of
G. CHRISTIAN WEISS,
Direction of Missions
Back to the Bible Broadcast
Lincoln, Nebraska

IF IN DOUBT, GO!

While at the beach in Jacksonville, Florida, one summer, I saw a lifeguard suddenly jump to his feet in his tower. He took the Red Cross flag out of its standard and waved it frantically so they could see him at the main life guard station. He then threw it to the ground, jumped down, grabbed a life buoy and rushed out into the water. With strong strokes he swam toward a man waving for help. In a few seconds sirens wailed as an ambulance came up and three other guards swam out to help. They rescued the man and gave him artificial respiration. Scores gathered around. All were deeply moved as the man was revived. This same scene was repeated several times that day, for the undertow was unusually strong.

Late that afternoon I went to the main station to say thanks as a private citizen for the dedication of these men. When I walked into the station I was struck by a sign on the wall in large red letters which read, IF IN DOUBT, GO! It struck me that this ought to be on the wall of every church and on the table of every heart as we see the multitudes around us and read the command of God to "Go!" That visitor in Sunday school or church, the neighbor, the friend across town, the postman, the paper boy, the one next to us on the plane, if in doubt whether he's a Christian or not, the Christian should "go" and "tell" that he too might have the opportunity of becoming a Christian.

The Favorite Illustration of
C. SUMNER WEMP, President
Southeastern Bible College
Birmingham, Alabama

MONKEYS TYPING A SHAKESPERIAN PLAY

My favorite illustration on the total failure of evolutionism comes from Bolton Davidheiser, *Evolution and Christian Faith*:

There is a well-known statement to the effect that if a million monkeys struck the keys of a million typewriters for a million years, they might by chance type a copy of a Shakesperian play. According to one version, the monkeys might type all of Shakespere's works. Another version postulates that they might type all of the books found in the British Museum. The point of all this is to show by analogy that if evolution is given enough time it might be able to produce through a process which involves chance all known forms of life starting from lifeless material.

If we assume some facts about the typing ability of monkeys we can treat these facts mathematically and see how convincing the analogy really is. Actually monkeys would soon tire of typing and would pursue more pleasing simian sports while the typewriters stood idle through most of the million years. If we assume, therefore, for the sake of the problem that these primates work diligently and find that they still are unable to produce anything of literary merit, the analogy will be shown to have no value. Indeed, the more extreme or absurd the assumptions we make favorable to their success, the more thoroughly the analogy will be discredited if the monkeys fail.

Instead of giving them standard typewriters let us give the monkeys simplified machines with only capital letters, seven punctuation marks, and a spacing key. Let us assume that each of the million monkeys types continuously twenty-four hours a day at the speed which the world's champion human typist was able to maintain for a few minutes — about twelve and a half keys per second. The only other assumption is that the monkeys type purely by chance and are as likely to strike any key as any other key.

To make their task simple, let us inquire how long it would be expected to take them to type not a whole Shakesperian play, but just the first line of Hamlet: *"BER: Who's there?"*

The answer is that if this experiment were repeated a number of times it would be expected to take them on the average 284,000,000,000 years.

To type the first verse of Genesis (or anything else of comparable length) would take them much longer.

The length of time it would be expected to require for them to type *"In the beginning God created the heaven and the earth"* is quite beyond our comprehension, but an illustration will help. Think of a large mountain which is solid rock. Once a year a bird comes and rubs its beak on the mountain, wearing away an amount equivalent to the finest grain of sand (about .0025 inch in diameter). At this rate of erosion the mountain would disappear very slowly, but when completely gone the monkeys would still just be warming up.

Think of a rock not the size of a mountain, but a rock larger than the whole earth. Try to think of a rock so large that if the earth were at its center its surface would touch the nearest star. This star is so far away that light from it takes more than four years to get here, traveling 186,000 miles every second. If a bird came once every million years and removed an amount equivalent to the finest grain of sand, four such rocks would be worn away before the champion super simians would be expected to type Genesis 1:1.

Of course this is quite fantastic, but it is evident that a million monkeys would never type a Shakesperian play in a million years. Evolutionists believe they are dealing with hundreds of millions of years and that almost anything could happen in this much time. However, some mathematicians have disagreed with this, using data furnished them by the evolutionists.

The Favorite Illustration of
JOHN C. WHITCOMB, JR.,
Professor of Old Testament
Grace Theological Seminary
Winona Lake, Indiana

FROM THE "NOW" GENERATION TO THE "FOREVER" GENERATION

The closing night of the Chicago Crusade last November a couple of hundred kids gathered around me after the service, and some of them had a lot of really deep theological questions they wanted answered.

Finally one boy elbowed his way through. His name was Rick. He said, "Look, gang, if you don't mind stepping aside, I have a long way to go and I've got to see that guy." "What's on your mind?" I asked him. Rick was trying to be a hippie. He wasn't quite old enough, but he was trying hard. He had the pants and the hairdo. But some boys of seventeen just don't have enough fuzz to grow a beard. He said, "You stood up there and you talked to us for forty-five minutes tonight from that old book, and you know and I know and I want all these kids to know that everything you gave us is at least two thousand or more years old. Isn't that right?" "That's right," I agreed. "Look here," he continued, "I'm a member of the now generation. How do you expect to communicate to the now generation stuff that's two thousand or more years old?" "Rick," I told him, "you've got a problem. If a guy is a member of the now generation, tomorrow he will be a member of the yesterday generation. Who wants to be a has-been?" "You got anything better to offer?" he asked. "Yes. Why don't you become a member of my generation? I'm a member of the forever generation." He said, "I never heard of that one." "You see, Rick," I told him, "this Book that is at least two thousand or more years old tells about the Lord Jesus who is the same yesterday and to-day (for the now generation) and forever. When you belong to Him you've got it made forever." Rick scratched his head and said, "You know, I think I buy that. How do you get into that forever generation?" Right there I told him, and Rick accepted Christ as his own.

How do I know Rick really got converted? He left by the back door, and when I followed about five minutes later, several people asked, "Who was that hippie you led to the Lord?" "How did you know?" I asked. "He told me about it on the way out."

> *The Favorite Illustration of*
> JACK WYRTZEN, Director
> Word of Life Fellowship, Inc.
> Schroon Lake, New York

GOD ANSWERS PRAYER FOR HAM

The experience I am about to relate took place in the city of Flint, Michigan, during the severe depression which began in October, 1929. I was then pastor of the Lincoln Park Methodist Church, which is located on Fenton Road, in the southwest section of the city. The factories were all closed, the banks were all closed, there was little or no work for anyone, anywhere. Men and women alike looked everywhere for work but there was no work to be had.

So I determined to do something about it. I was radio broadcasting a half-hour gospel program each morning over Station WFDF and my Sunday services as well. I knew that there were scores of well-to-do farmers living in Gratiot County in which the city of Flint is located. So I appealed to all the farmers who could, and who would, to donate potatoes, beans, and other vegetables. I told them I planned to open a soup kitchen and make a rich soup which would be given free to all who would come for it.

A vacant building nearby was donated, several large kettles, each holding 100 gallons were bought; stores, meat markets and bakeries were contacted, and all promised to help. The farmers responded generously, giving dry beans and other vegetables. Two experienced cooks were engaged and soon the food program was under way. At 4:30 each afternoon families would come with their containers. The bakeries donated day-old bread and rolls, the dairies furnished skim milk, and the meat markets soup bones, bologna, and meat with which we made a rich soup which was given free each day.

Knowing that General Motors owned several hundred acres of rich land near to the city the thought then came to me, "This rich land is lying vacant, growing up in weeds; if you contacted the officials of General Motors, perhaps they would let you use this land to raise food to feed these hungry people." So I went to see Mr. Knudson, who was then president of the big Buick factory which was closed. He secured permission for me to use 487 acres of this land, so I bought nine second-hand tractors. I secured the farming equipment we needed. I used the men of the city who had farming experience. We plowed the land, planted it, and raised enough food to feed the entire city.

Now, to tell you the story of how God wonderfully answered prayer. Each morning my trucks would go to different parts of the city and pick up the men. Each morning I would serve the men a good breakfast of oatmeal, bread and rolls, skim milk or coffee, before they were taken to the farms to work. Lunch would be carried to them at noon, and a hot dinner was ready for them when they returned from the farms in the evening. They were given a meal of cooked vegetables, bologna, skim milk or coffee, bread and rolls. After the meal the men were given bread, milk, bologna, and soup to take home to their families.

Each morning I would conduct a short gospel service with the men before they were taken to the farms. All nationalities were represented in this group. One morning one of my cooks who was an atheist said to me, "Doc [the men all called me "Doc"], do you really believe God answers prayer?"

"Of course God answers prayer. I have had many prayers answered. This very kitchen and its program is an answer to prayer."

The cook continued, "If so, I wish you would ask God to send us some ham. We have been eating bologna now week after week; all the meat we have is bologna; it's bologna,

bologna; I have been eating bologna until it sticks out of my ears. I never want to see another ring of bologna as long as I live! Please pray to your God asking Him to send us some ham."

I looked at the man. The large dining room was filled to capacity. I knew they all felt like my atheist cook. I stood on a chair before them and said, "Men, how many of you believe that God could send us some ham if I were to ask Him for it? All who believe God could and would send us some ham, raise your hands." Nearly every hand was raised; these men were not unbelievers.

I continued, "Now I am asking you another question: How many of you believe that if I were to pray, asking God to send us a supply of ham for supper tonight, that God would answer *now,* and send us ham for supper?" Only a few hands were now raised. The men knew the scarcity of ham in the market.

I made a simple prayer something like this: "Dear Heavenly Father, you know we have been eating bologna for weeks; we are indeed thankful for it, but we would like some ham for a change. We know there is still plenty of ham in the country. If it please Thee, send us some ham and we will thank Thee for it. I ask this in Jesus' Name, Amen."

Breakfast was over and the men climbed up on the trucks and left for work. I returned to my office. As I entered, Joy Rowley, my secretary, said, "Dr. Zoller, the freight agent just called. He has asked you to call him at once, it is an emergency; here is his phone number." Wondering what the emergency could be, I called the number. The agent answered. He said, "Dr. Zoller, Swift and Company, of Chicago, were sending a carload of ham through the city but the refrigeration has gone bad. The car is now standing on the siding. The ham is in perfect condition, but it must be cared for *at once.* If you can use it, Swift and Company will donate it to you to feed the needy in the city!"

Could we use it? Could we? What a wonderful answer to prayer this was! "Charlie," I answered, "Wire Swift and Company immediately that we gratefully accept this carload of ham; it is a definite answer to prayer. I will write them our thanks later. Arrangements will be made immediately to care for the entire carload."

I hurried back to the soup kitchen. Imagine the surprise of the cooks when they learned how quickly God had answered prayer. I immediately sent two trucks for the ham. I told the cooks to use only one kettle for soup, to fill the other kettle with ham, and to boil each ham for a half-hour. We would give each man a ham to take home to his family, and all who came for soup would be given a ham.

Soon the smell of boiling ham filled the air. We could smell it for nearly a block. As people passed by they said, "Doc must have obtained ham somewhere, for they are certainly boiling ham!" And when the men returned from work in the evening, as they drew near the kitchen, they began to cry out, "Ham, I smell ham, we are going to have ham for supper, the Lord has certainly answered prayer and sent us some ham!" Little did the men know and realize that God had indeed answered prayer.

We did have ham for supper that night. Our cooks placed large platters filled with sliced ham before the men. When the men were all seated ready to eat I stood on a chair before them and said, "Men, God has indeed answered prayer!" I told them what had happened, that we had a full carload of ham, enough to have ham time and again. I told them that there was a free ham for every man to take home to his family.

My atheist cook was sitting before me. After a grateful prayer of thanksgiving he looked up into my face, and with tears in his eyes he said, "Doc, I believe! I tell you, I believe!" And he did believe, for he was a changed man from that hour. Later he decided to preach the gospel. He went to the Moody Bible Institute for training and he is preaching the blessed gospel today. Yes, God *does* indeed answer prayer!

The Favorite Illustration of
DR. JOHN ZOLLER
Radio Pastor
New Era, Michigan

INDEX

Titles of the Favorite Illustrations